# Paper Dolls

### EARLY HISTORICAL RARITIES TO POPULAR CULTURE EDITIONS
#### 1790-1940

By Florence Theriault

In consultation with Sheryl Jaeger

Theriault's
Gold Horse Publishing

© 2006 Theriault's Gold Horse Publishing. All rights reserved.

No part of this book may be reproduced or utilized in any form or by any means, electronic or mechanical, including photocopying, recording, or by any information retrieval system, without permission, in writing, from the author or the publisher.

To order additional copies contact:
Dollmasters
PO Box 2319
Annapolis, MD 21404
Tel. 800-966-3655, Fax 410-571-9605
www.dollmasters.com

Design by Travis Hammond
Photography by Gerald Nelson

$49
ISBN: 1-931503-42-7
Printed in Hong Kong

# This paper doll collection auctioned by Theriault's of Annapolis, Maryland, November 12, 2006.
*www.theriaults.com.*

# Table of Contents

Chapter I. European Paper Dolls 1790-1860 — 6

Chapter II. American Paper Dolls 1800-1870 — 47

Chapter III. 1880-WWI Era — 60

Chapter IV. European Paper Dolls 1790-1860 — 94

Chapter V. The New Century — 108

Chapter VI. Postcard & Greeting Card Paper Dolls — 120

Chapter VII. Advertising Paper Dolls — 124

Chapter VIII. Post WWI — 145

# The Exceptional Paper Doll Collection of Shirley Fischer

The paper doll collection of Shirley Fischer reflects the life-long ardent pursuit of a passionate and intelligent collector, and ranges from early historical rarities so precious many collectors have not known of their existence, to popular culture icons. So distinguished was she in the paper doll field that in 2004, she befittingly received the special award of Distinguished Paper Doll Ambassador. Yet despite this steady and tireless involvement in the paper doll community, in paper preservation organizations and historical museums, despite her mentoring of new collectors, despite her research into the unknown and un-identified, she was essentially a private, non-boastful collector and few knew the extent of her collection. Until now. Until this catalog.

The collection spans 150 years, from 1790 through the 1940's. It is likely that few collections exist today with the extent of early historical rarities as the Fischer Collection.

It includes early dolls from Germany, France and England and virtually all of the early American paper dolls. She sought the rare and unusual but also understood the importance of popular culture. She made a concerted effort to collect at least one set of paper dolls of every American maker. Her collection includes envelope and box sets, bound books, advertising sets, and magazine and newspaper series, and sweeps from the Complete Paper Doll Family of Anson Randolph to the one-of-a-kind artist proof of "Mary Elizabeth" by Queen Holden.

Among the early English rarities are Fuller's 1811 Protean Figure and Metamorphic Costumes, Dickerson's 1820 Dresses Worn at the Coronation of His Majesty George IV, 1830's "Belinda at Her Toilet" with miniature wooden Psyche mirror, Izzard's 1820's "The Sovereign's of England from Henry IV to George IV", and the 1830's Ackermann boxed set of "La Poupee Modele" (an historical curiosity that opens new debate concerning the French versions of this same-named paper doll). Superb early French boxed rarities include the 1830's Tagliani, Doyen's 1826 Le Paravent ou Les Petites Acteurs, 1821 Les Metamorphoses d'Auguste, La Coquette, Le Petite Costumier, L'Ecole des Modes, Psyche, La Poupee Modele, and others including an exceptional pair of fireplace fans with "hidden" paper doll costumes. Early German paper dolls include 1790 set of Englische Puppe by Stahl of Nuremberg, 1803 set by Bestelmeier, 1791 man and woman dolls by Wallis, and mid-19th century boxed sets including The Masquerade, The Genteel Boy and His Doings, The 12 Months of the Year in Boy's Dress, and The Season of the Crinoline among many others. Early American paper dolls feature works by Anson Randolph, Peter Thomson, Chromatic Printing, R.A. Hobbs, Joseph Shaw, Clark Austin and Smith, Crosby, Nichols and Co, Degens, Estes & Co, and McLoughlin.

Paper dolls of popular culture range from an extensive collection of newspaper and magazine supplements to Little Colonel Story Book (autographed) and Mary Ware paper doll book, from 100's of very rare advertising novelty paper doll sets such as Mapl-Sisters Doll House Rooms and Paper Dolls to Queen Holden treasures, from an uncut Alice in Wonderland with Cut-out Pictures book to exquisite uncut books from Stokes/Tucker. There are postcard paper dolls, mechanical greeting cards, scrap, articulated string paper dolls, articulated animal paper dolls, and die-cut Santa's and holiday trees with "surprise" paper dolls. There are the classics ranging from Raphael Tuck to the Woolworth dolls, from Selchow & Richter to Saalfield.

It is a gift to the collecting world when one-person collections are presented uniquely and in their entirety. Often even the collector herself fails to recognize the prevailing vision that guides her choices. Only when the collection is finally viewed through the eyes of other collectors do patterns emerge. Thus we are amused at the mechanical curtseying girl (#18) and then realize that the simple mechanical paper pull is the same as 20th century sleeping eye paper dolls. The rare English profile dolls of #1 are echoed a century and a half later in Queen Holden's Glamour Girl. We can see the vision of Shirley Fischer even though we fail at putting it into words.

Collectors choose their paper dolls for many reasons: a study of fashion, an appreciation for the illustration and art work, an intrigue with the artistic devices employed in doll construction and costume adherence, or for the perspective of social history that many offer. Or they simply choose them for the same reason that Sally Blinn, a young girl of 5 in the mid-1950's chose her paper dolls: "I just loved them. I could take them with me everywhere, I could dream of who they were and where they were going and what they could wear. I could make my own costumes to add to the store-bought ones. They were my friends. They were my dreams."

# Chapter I. European Paper Dolls 1790-1860

**1. Exceptionally Rare 1790 German Profile Paper Dolls "Englische Puppe" by Stahl of Nuremberg**
A marbled paper folio with hand-lettered title "Englische Puppe" contains two 5" x 8" rose paper folios with labeled interior sleeves, containing hand-drawn and colored paper dolls depicting a lady and gentleman in profile poses, facing each other. The lady owns four costumes along with five additional skirts allowing a wide variety of costume variations, and 8 different very elaborate hats. The gentleman owns seven jackets or greatcoats, one vest, one suit, four pairs of pants, boots, sword, one hat, and three jabots, designed to be mixed in various ways. The rose envelopes are labeled "La Pouppee anglaise a diversified modes, Habillement, Coifures et port d'habits" by "J.L.Stahl, Nurnb" and the exterior envelope contains instructions (German). Excellent condition, beautiful art work and coloring of costumes. Germany, Stahl, circa 1790. $4000/6500

Paper Dolls

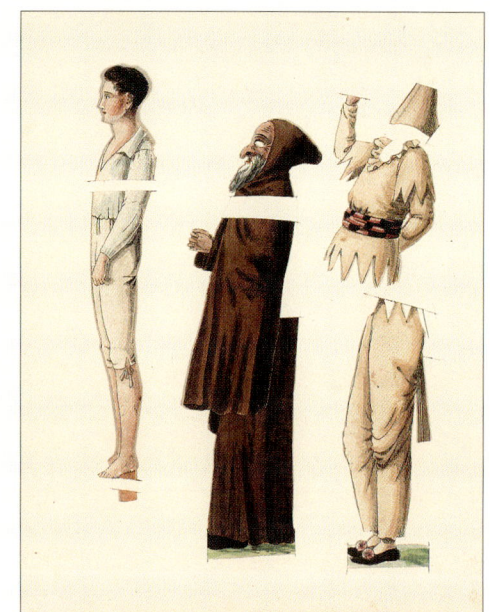

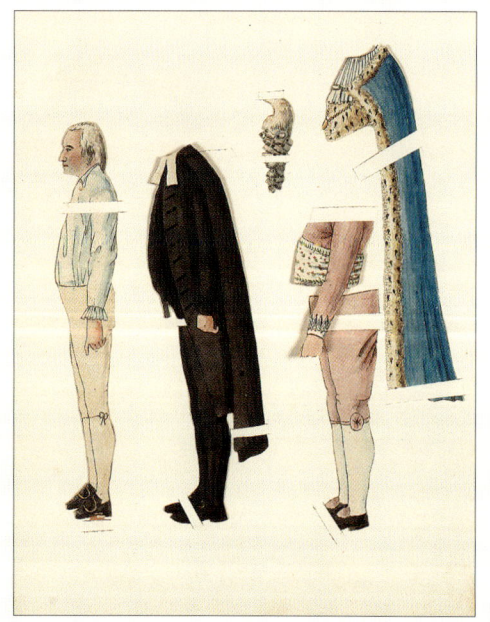

Paper Dolls

**2. Circa 1800, Very Fine German Profile Paper Dolls by Bestelmeier**
Three paper dolls depicting men in profile pose are presented in a blue parchment folio, including 5.5" aged gentlemen and 5.5" young man with 11 interchangeable costumes designed to fit either man, 7 hats, periwig, and 3 unusual face masks with attached hats; along with a smaller 5" man, profile posed for standing or horseback riding, having six variations of military costume, 10 hats or helmets, flag, and 6 fancy saddles. Each is hand drawn and hand-colored. Excellent condition with beautifully preserved water-colors. Attributed to Bestelmeier, Germany, circa 1800. $4000/6000

**3. Circa 1815, Uncut Sheet of French Paper Dolls**
The 10.5" x 14" uncut sheet features four paper dolls, each with centerfold to create a dimensional look when assembled, and with additional back views of arms with accessories. The paper dolls and accessories are hand-colored, and extremely rare to find especially in uncut state. French, attributed to Chanvin, circa 1815. $200/300

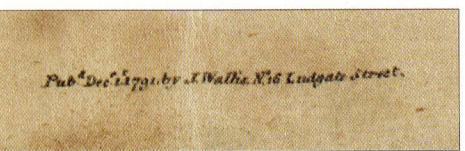

**4. 1791 English Profile Paper Dolls of Lady and Gentleman by J. Wallis**
The heads of a lady and gentleman are attached to long paper strip designed for costume attachment. The lady owns four gowns and the gentleman has five costumes. Each is hand-drawn and delicately water-colored with exquisite detail of accessories. Each costume and doll is marked with tiny signature "Pub.Dec 20 1791 by J. Wallis No 16 Ludgate Street". Excellent condition. England, 1791. $2000/3000

**5. Circa 1820, Dutch Paper Doll Book "Louize" by J. Guykens**
A small grey paper covered book, 4" x 5", titled "De Weldadige Louize" contains a story featuring young Louize, along with an uncut card of Louize as paper doll and six costumes with attached hats to accompany each story line. The set is similar to the Fuller series of England created about the same period. Very good condition, some light spotting on doll card. Published by Joh. Guykens of Amsterdam, circa 1820. $800/1200

**6. Circa 1820, Dutch Paper Doll Book "Willem" by J. Guykens**
A companion series to #4 featuring the adventures of "Schalksche Willem", comprising the storybook with uncut card of Willem and four costumes, designed to accompany the story line. Very good condition, some light spotting on doll card. Published by Jon. Guykens of Amsterdam, circa 1820. $800/1200

**7. Extremely Rare and Fine 1811 English "The Protean Figure and Metamorphic Costumes" by S&J Fuller**

An exterior folio with illustration of the Greek God Proteus (Protean) arising from the sea is beautifully lettered "The Protean Figure and Metamorphic Costumes", and contains a 17½" x 11" heavy parchment background of English country scene, the sea in the background, rendered in delicate watercolors, and a bound book with instructions on use and 12 intricately folded paper envelopes, each containing a hand-colored costume of four or more elements. The hand-colored paper doll is a profile view of a handsome young man of the Romantic Era. Each costume envelope has a paper label with elegantly labeled name of the costume within: Walking Dress, Mourning Suit, Turkish Costume, Quaker's Habit, Officer's Uniform (Land Forces), Full Dress in the Year 1700, Monk Habit, Naval Uniform, German Hussar, Knight in Full Armour, Gentlemen's Evening Costume, French Uniform

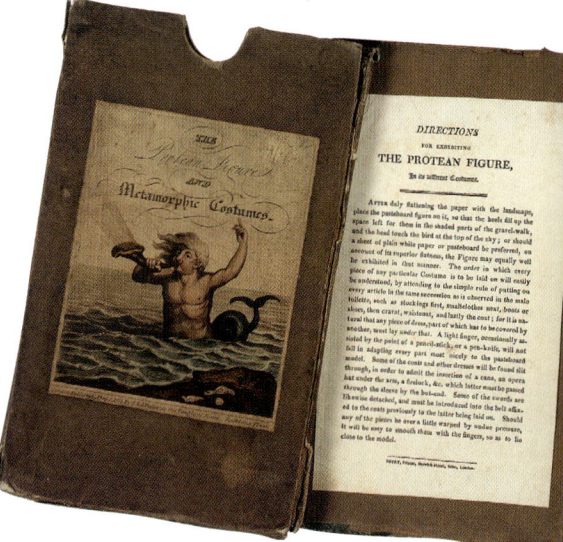

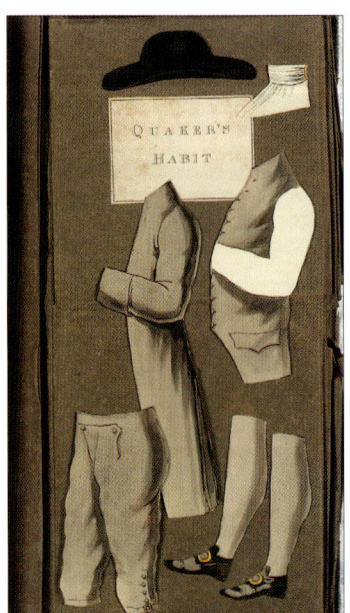
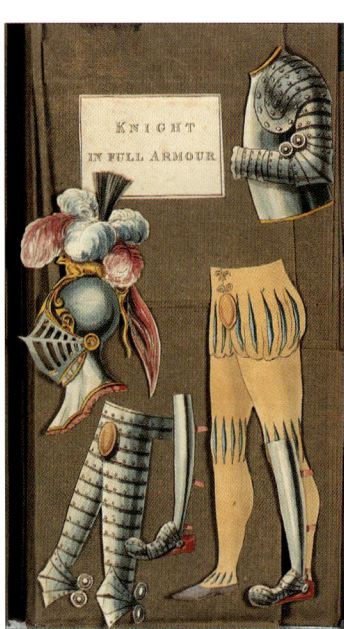

   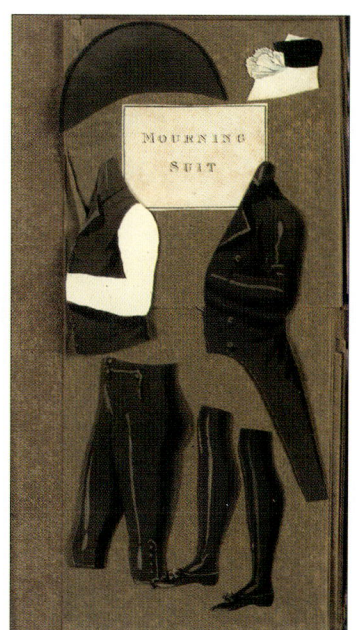

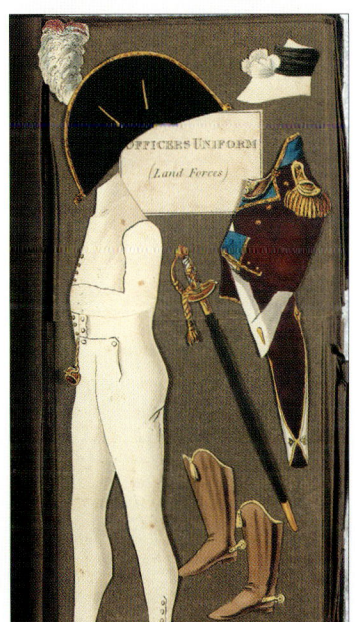 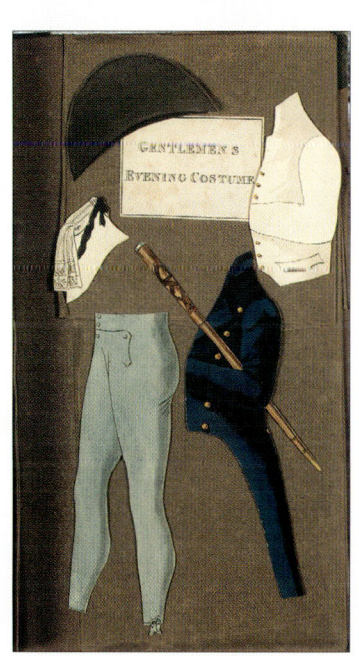  

(Imperial Guard). The inside front cover of the book has "Directions for Exhibiting The Protean Figure" including details of where to place the man on the background (his feet in the shadows of the gravel walk, and his head touching the bird in the sky), and the sensible advice of how to dress the doll, i.e. the same order in which a man would dress himself. The name of Suury (sic) Printer, Berwick Street, Soho, London appears on the inside cover. Excellent condition. S&J Fuller, England, 1811. $6500/8500

*Historical Note: The Greek God Proteus (Protean) was characterized by a remarkable ability to change shape and appearance – hence the paper doll costume changes. In English literature and arts he had been a prominent symbolic figure for centuries in works ranging from Milton to Shakespeare, and, more relevant to this work, Protean appeared in a romantic sonnet of William Wordsworth, published just 3 years prior to the appearance of "The Protean Figure and Metamorphic Costumes".*

Paper Dolls

**8. Romantic Era French Hand-Colored Overlay Paper Doll in Folio** A hand-colored bust of a beautiful woman of the Romantic era is centered on a 5" x 4.5" pasteboard card, and can be "dressed" by overlay of any of the eight images with watercolor costume and cut-out face. The overlays include costumes of Swiss, Cherbourg and Bordeaux, as well as high fashion Parisian attire of the years 1816, 1825 and 1826, each identified in delicate script at the bottom of the card. The set is contained in original folio with marbleized paper. Excellent condition, moderate wear on folio. French, circa 1826. $2000/3000

**9. 1820's English Paper Dolls "The Sovereigns of England from Henry VII to His Present Most Gracious Majesty George IV" in Boxed Set**
A fine wooden box, 7.5" x 4.5", with printed paper label on its lid depicting a monarch in coronation robes contains within its paper-lined interior a book detailing 16 English monarchs with a description of the physical appearance and reign of each, along with a numbered costume on heavy pasteboard and having self base with vignette elements for each monarch (the numbers corresponding to the booklet chapters). Included are two hand-drawn (not original) faces, 6 hats and 2 crowns. The costumes are each initialed W.H.B. and the booklet bears the mark of James Izzard, London. Very fine condition of costumes, one end of box lid missing. James Izzard, London, early 1820's. $6000/8500

*Historical Note: the set was presented shortly after the 1821 coronation of George IV and provides an entertaining perspective on the propaganda power of a (presumably) child's plaything. Whereas the writer described earlier monarchs in such terms as "his character was an odd mixture of sense and folly" (James I) and "the length and narrowness of her face prevented her from having any just pretensions to beauty" (Elizabeth), George IV was described as "tall and extremely well proportioned and is esteemed handsome...his kindness, affability and condescension endear him to all".*

Paper Dolls

**10. 1811 English Paper Doll and Book "Ellen, the Naughty Girl Remembered"**
Protected inside its original slipcase is a 4" x 5" book with brown paper covers and beautifully lettered title. The 19 interior pages tell the story of Ellen in nine scenes, and to accompany the scenes there are nine cut-out hand-colored vignettes of Ellen in various costumes. Also included are five separate hats and one head. Excellent condition with beautifully preserved vignettes and rich colors, exterior folio has some aging. Printed for S&J Fuller, Temple of Fancy, by D.N. Shury, Berwick Street, Soho, London. Dated 1811 on title page. $700/900

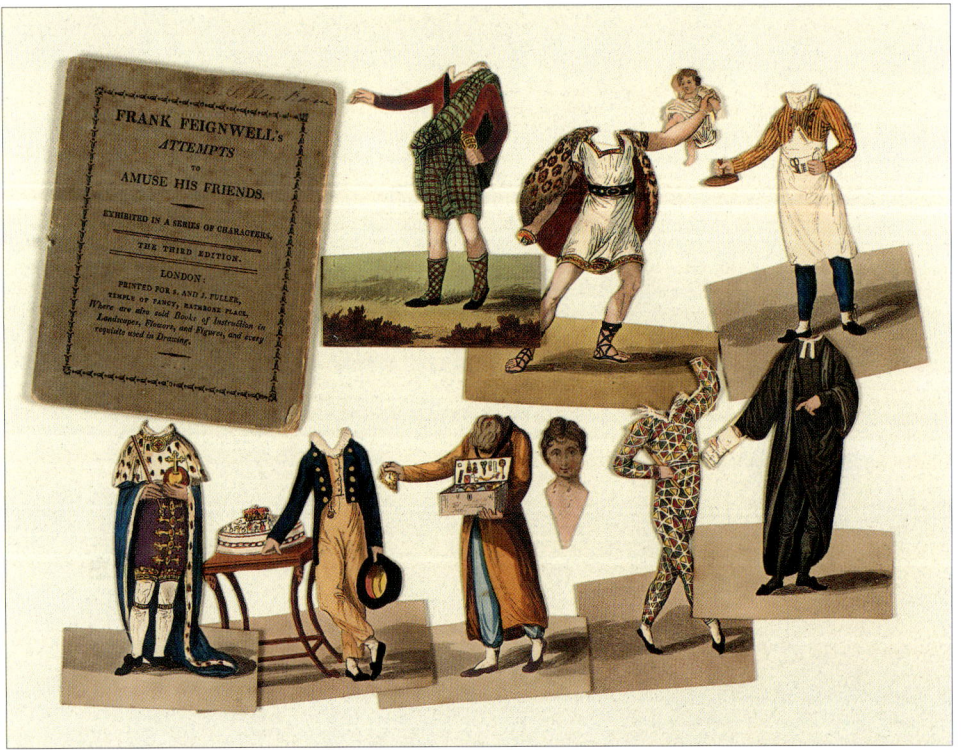

**11. 1811 English Paper Doll and Book "Frank Feignwell's Attempts to Amuse His Friends"**
A brown paper covered 4" x 5" book, protected by exterior folio, tells the amusing antics of young Frank as he disguises himself in various ways ranging from harlequin to barrister to peddler. Accompanying the chapters are eight cut-out hand-colored vignettes of Frank in costumes to match the stories, and one head. Costumes are excellent; head, folio and book covers have age spotting. Printed for S&J Fuller, Temple of Fancy, by D.N. Shury, Berwick Street, Soho, London. Dated 1811 on title page. $700/900

**12. 1810 English Paper Doll and Book "The History of Little Fanny"**
An original grey/brown slip case encloses a matching 4" x 5" book detailing The History of Little Fanny as she learns to be humble and demure. One head, 4 hats and 7 cut-out hand-colored vignettes accompany the chapter stories, each with different costumes and accessories, one holding a doll. Very fine condition throughout. Printed for S&J Fuller, Temple of Fancy, by D.N. Shury, Berwick Street, Soho, London. Dated 1810 on title page. $500/800

**13. 1810 English Paper Doll and Book "The History and Adventures of Little Henry"**
A green paper-covered 4" x 5" book details stories of Little Henry, kidnapped from his wealthy home, and finally returned to his beloved family. Seven cut-out hand-colored vignettes with different costumes, along with two separate hats, accompany the stories. Cut-outs excellent, folio slipcase lacking, head included but not original. Printed for S&J Fuller, Temple of Fancy, by D.N. Shury, Berwick Street, Soho, London. Dated 1810 on title page. $500/700

**14. Circa 1810, Extremely Rare French Fireplace Fan with Paper Doll and Costumes**
A 15" heavy card paper fireplace fan with carved ebony handle has a hand-painted garden scene of a country chateau. The figure of a woman is attached to the background as though she is walking down the path. On the reverse of the fan is a red paper envelope inscribed "costumes francais" that contains six exquisite hand-drawn costumes (four with attached millinery) that the lady can wear as she chooses. Excellent condition excepting neck repair. French, circa 1810. $1500/3000

**15. Circa 1810, Rare and Fine French Fireplace Fan with Paper Doll and Costumes** Possibly a companion to #14, excepting variation of background scene, here a forest with shepherd and flock in the background, and variation of woman paper doll figure. The envelope at the back is labeled "costumes etranger" and contains six hand-drawn folklore costumes of European locales, each inscribed with name of costume on the reverse side. Excellent condition. French, circa 1810. $1500/3000

Paper Dolls

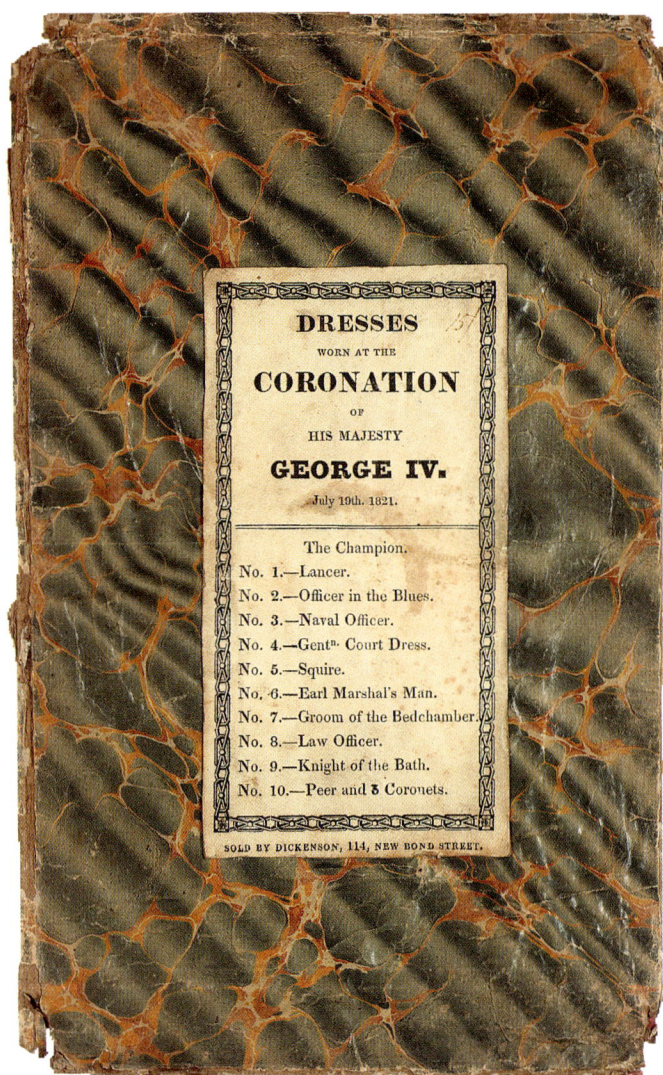

**16. An 1821 Extremely Rare English Paper Doll Set "Dresses Worn at the Coronation of His Majesty George IV"**

An 11" x 7" marbled-paper folio with original label that details the ten costumes included within, viz Officer in the Blues, Groom of the Bedchamber, Law Officer, and seven others, contains all of the listed costumes along with a knight in armor on horseback (two parts) and one head. Each costume is on heavy card paper and is exquisitely hand-drawn and water-colored with fine nuance of shading and detail. The folio is labeled "Sold by Dickenson, 114, New Bond Street" and dated July 19, 1821. $3000/4500

*Historical Note: King George IV of England was crowned in 1820; he is most remembered for his extravagant life style as these costumes indicate. Excellent condition, some wear to folio cover. England, 1821.*

Paper Dolls

**17. An 1814 English Paper Doll and Book "Cinderella" by S&J Fuller**
A paper bound miniature book, 5" x 4", recounts in "beautifully versified" form the favored fairy tale, and was designed to be read while playing with the paper dolls, vignettes and accessories that illustrate the tale, comprising six costume scenes including the wedding, and Cinderella's coach and horses (in two sections). An inscription inside the front cover reads "To my dear little niece Constance Foley". S&J Fuller, Temple of Fancy, Rathbone Place, London, 1814. Structure and lovely delicate colors of paper dolls and scenes well preserved, coachman's head missing, one hand missing, stain on book cover. England, 1814. $800/1100

**18. An Articulated English Paper Doll Card "Very Well, Your Honor"**
Attached to a heavy paper card with hand-drawn feet and shading, is an articulated figure of a young maiden with hand-colored costume and features. When the tab at the base of the card is pulled, the girl appears to both curtsy and nod her head. Inscribed at the base is the message "Very well, your honor". Excellent condition. England, early 19th century. $200/300

**19. An 1821 French Miniature Paper Doll Book "*Les Metamorphoses D'Auguste*"**
A miniature book, 5" x 3.5", with rich silk-like cover, recounts the story of young Auguste in six chapters, each entailing the need of a different costume for Auguste. In an envelope incorporated into the book is a heavy cardboard card with an engraved figure of Auguste, along with six different one-piece costumes that correspond to the various stories; the original slipcase is also included. Published in Paris, 1821, by Chez Nepveu. Passage des Panorama No.26. Doll is uncut, and costumes are complete and excellent. Book covers, spine and slipcase are worn. France, 1821. $1800/2800

**20. Early Viennese Paper Doll Set "*Vier Geschwister in Costums*" by Muller**
A thin wooden box, 8" x 5.5", with marbleized paper cover is inside a book-shaped matching cover with old paper label "Vier Geschwister in Costums", and contains four 6" paper dolls (2 men, 2 women) with 16 hand-colored double-sided costumes and 16 hats. Marked "Wien, in der Kunsthandlung des H.F. Muller, am Kohnmarkt, No1149". Excellent condition except outer box has some fading, wear. Dolls and costumes excellent. H. F. Muller, Vienna, circa 1840. $1500/2200

Paper Dolls

Paper Dolls

**21. Very Rare Viennese "Mythologie Pour La Jeunesse" by Muller**
A beautifully printed marbled paper folio with appliqué paper scroll "Mythologie", 9.5" x 6", contains a 72 page book, written in both German and French, detailing the writer's purpose: to teach mythology to his children by means of paper dolls with changeable costumes that represent the features of various Greek or Roman Gods. Included are 2 marble-paper envelopes each containing a heavy cardboard paper doll representing a female or male deity, each with 7 different costumes (and 2 head-dresses for the female). The name of the god or goddess represented in ink-script noted on the back of each costume. Excellent condition of dolls and costumes, wrappers a bit worn. H.F. Muller, Vienna, 1841. $4500/6500

**22. Boxed German Paper Doll Set, "Costumes of Man of All Centuries"**
Featuring a handsome young man, single-sided, along with eight costumes and eight hats depicting costumes from past centuries. The costumes are double-sided, with black back and are enhanced with egg wash. Contained in original box, 7" x 9", with four-language titles, and a rich court scene that depicts four of the costumes inside. Marked "Verl. Eigth. G.M.". Dolls and costumes excellent and complete, box a bit worn. Printed in Germany, mid-19th century, probably Eigenthum. $1500/3000

**23. Circa 1835, Extremely Rare French Paper Doll Set, "Taglioni" in Original Box**

Featuring Marie Taglioni, the renowned ballerina of the European Romantic era, was born in Sweden, rose to prominence in Italian and Parisian ballets, beginning in 1832 in La Sylphide in which she danced the entire performance en pointe. She retired from performing in 1847 but remained a guiding spirit of the Paris Ballet for several decades more. The paper doll set highlights costumes from her most famous performances, and the boxed set includes the double-sided doll, nine-double-sided costumes, nine head-dresses (including one elaborately cut dimensional head dress in miniature box), along with maple wood stand, and original list of the operas and costumes included. The set is contained in its original box, 8" x 10.5", having embossed rose sides, gilt edging, and delicately engraved lid portraying the dancer and the name "Taglioni". Excellent condition with vibrant costume colors. Few examples of the very rare luxury set are known to exist, made more remarkable by the fine state of preservation. France, circa 1835. $3500/5500

Paper Dolls

### 24. Early Boxed German Paper Doll Set "The Masquerade"

Featuring four paper dolls (two men, two women) along with 17 theatre double-sided (back blank) costumes and 14 different heads with variations in coiffures and head-dress. The rich detail of the costumes is enhanced by egg wash lustre. Contained in original box, 8" x 11", with three-language titles, decorative paper sides, embossed gilt edging, and a rich lithographed design on the lid featuring nine of the actual costumes. Marked "Bei F. Fechner in Guben". Excellent condition with slight roughness to base of dolls and minor edge wear on box. Germany, circa 1850. $3500/5500

**25. Early Boxed German Paper Doll Set "The Noble Young Lady"**
Featuring a demurely posed young lady "in romantic Costume of the Middle Ages with 8 magnificent dresses and grand vistas" according to description on the box lid. The set includes eight Medieval style double-sided (blank back) elaborate gowns (most incorporating an accessory such as scepter, mandolin, or such) and four hats or head-dresses. Also included is a three-part folding screen with richly draped curtains centering a window with "grand vistas". Contained in original four-language box, 7" x 9", with a finely detailed engraving of Medieval-era women in a bucolic setting. Marked "Verlag Eigenthum C.M.". Excellent condition, beautifully preserved egg-wash lustre enhances the rich colors, box a bit worn. Germany, mid-19th century. $3500/5000

**26. 1850's French Boxed Set of Paper Dolls "L'Ecole des Modes"**
A heavy pasteboard box with lid engraving depicting six fashionable women admiring fabrics and millinery in a well-appointed salon, is edged in richly embossed gilded papers and lettered "L'Ecole des Modes". The box contains one paper doll arranged in modest pose, along with eight hand-colored double-sided fashionable gowns and 3 bonnets. Excellent condition, slight edge wear on box. France, 1850's. $1200/1800

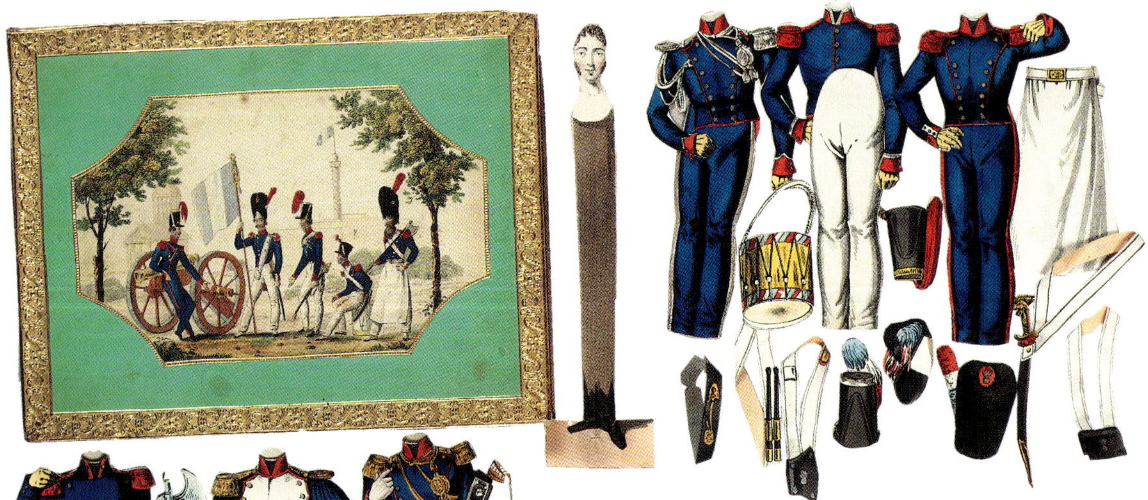

**27. 1840's French Boxed Set of Paper Doll Soldiers**
A heavy pasteboard box whose lid depicts an early engraved scene of five French soldiers in regimental uniforms has embossed gilt edging, and contains within a 7" stick body double-sided paper doll man, along with six uniforms and an extravagant array of military accessories including rifles, drums, sabers, helmets and other head wear. Excellent condition. France, 1840's. $2000/3000

**28. 1840's Rare French Boxed Set "Le Petit Costumier" with Theatrical Figures**
A pasteboard box with engraving of familiar French theatrical figures such as Harlequin, along with fashionably dressed ladies are riding in an open topped carriage being driven by Polichinelle. The box is labeled "Le Petit Costumier, A Paris". Inside is contained one paper doll, designed to be costumed as man or woman, three costumes for man (harlequin, Polichinelle and Bon Vivant), and three costumes for women including Pierrette and a fashionable lady's gown whose arms are holding two early puppet theatre dolls. Excellent condition, box lid a bit age darkened. France, 1840's. $1500/2500

**29. 1850's French Boxed Set of Five Dolls "Les Jeux Enfantins"**
A heavy pasteboard box with hand-tinted engraving on the lid depicting two mothers and four children at play in a park setting, titled "Les jeux Enfantins, Children's Games" contains five double-sided paper dolls: two mothers, boy, girl and toddler. There are 9 double-sided costumes with egg-wash finish (at least one for each doll) and four hats. Very good condition, box lid darkened, one mother bent at neck and base. The box is labeled H. Duru, editeur and lithographed by H. Jannin. France, circa 1850. $1000/1400

### 30. Extremely Rare 1826 French Paper Doll with Scenery "Le Paravent, Les Petite Acteurs"

A pasteboard box with delicate engraving on the lid depicting the contents, along with title, and embossed gilded paper borders contains within a four-part heavy board folding screen (the "Paravent") with bucolic scene, along with two paper dolls in the Romantic style (boy and girl), each on wooden stand, and 9 costumes with attached head wear. Included is the original "script" for the play to be performed; each of the players corresponds to one of the nine costumes. The script book is dated Paris 1826, published by G. Doyen. Excellent condition, minimal foxing on box lid. France, 1826. $4000/5500

### 31. 1840's English Boxed Paper Dolls "Belinda at Her Toilet" with Mirror

A 6" x 4.5" maple wood box with engraving on the lid portraying Belinda and her lady admiring Belinda's new gown as Belinda gazes into a mirror, contains a miniature wooden mirror (a duplicate to the cover image), double-sided paper doll with wooden base, 8 double-sided gowns with elaborate detail (one is the same as that shown on the lid image), 3 hats, and a paisley shawl. Despite their rare petite size, the costumes are exquisitely detailed, and the hinged Psyche mirror, with gilded frame, is arranged in a beautifully carved walnut stand. Excellent condition overall, neck bend, feet worn. The inclusion of miniature doll furniture in the set is an extremely rare variation. English, circa 1840. $1500/2500

**32. 1850's German Boxed Set of Paper Dolls "The 12 Months of the Year in Boy's Dress"**
A 7" x 6" pasteboard box with elaborate cover image and decorations has 3-language title (English, German, and French) and embossed paper border. Inside is 1 paperdoll of a young lad and 8 additional boy's costumes each presented in vignette form with background and accessories to enhance their motif. The costumes are spot varnished against the backgrounds, enhancing their vibrancy. Excellent condition overall, neck bend. Germany, circa 1850. $2000/2700

34  Paper Dolls

**33. 1850's German Boxed Set of Paper Dolls "The Genteel Boy and His Doings"**
A 7"x 9" pasteboard box with ornate cover design including bird and animal trimmed border encircling an image of seven children playing with the paper doll set; the image depicts the actual paper doll wearing one of the costumes included, and several of the children in the image are wearing costumes that are also included in the set. The box has 3 language titles and embossed gold edging. Inside is a double-sided paper boy along with 8 double-sided costumes and 4 hats, each with spot egg-shell varnish and each costume in vignette background. Excellent condition of contents except neck bend, box worn. German, circa 1850. $2000/3000

Paper Dolls

**34. 1840's German Paper Dolls, in Dance Costumes, by Fieure & Sauer**
A pair of double-sided paper dolls depict a Romantic Era young boy and girl in dancing pose, along with double-sided costumes for each (5 for boy, 4 and 1 hat for girl) depicting traditional costumes for various dances. The costumes have added vibrancy from varnish touches and each is arranged in background vignette. Excellent condition with vibrant costume colors, neck and leg bends on dolls. Germany, Fieure & Sauer, circa 1840's. $800/1100

**35. Remarkable 1860 French Set of Paper Dolls "La Mode Depuis 100 Ans"**
An extensive set of small paper dolls and their costumes, designed to illustrate fashion history from 1760-1860, is highlighted by the original printed inventory list describing each costume in detail. Included are four double-sided paper dolls (2 men, 2 women), four wooden stands, 11 double-sided gowns, 11 women's hats, 12 men's costumes, 6 men's hats. The set is preserved in an antique French candy box of the 1860 era. Excellent condition. French, circa 1860. $2000/2500

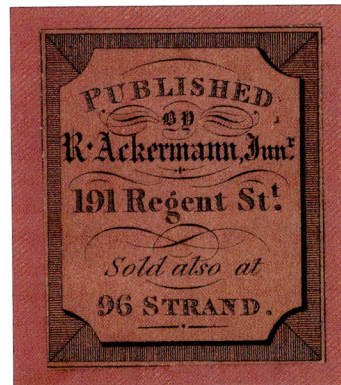

**36. Superb 1830's English Boxed Paper Doll "La Poupee Modele" by Ackermann**
8.5" doll. A heavy pasteboard box whose cover has an engraving of the paper doll in period costume, gilded paper edging, and lettered "La Poupee Modele" contains one double-sided doll in lingerie, on self base, along with six double-sided gowns and two hats. The gowns have gilded hand-painted details such as belt buckles or brooches. The doll base and the inside box lid are labeled "Published by R. Ackermann, Jun. 191 Regent St, Sold Also at 96 Strand". Excellent condition, some age darkening of box, contents beautifully preserved. Ackermann, England, circa 1830's. $2000/3000

Paper Dolls

**37. 1860's Very Rare and Opulent German Boxed Paper Doll "Season of the Crinoline"** 8.5" doll. A 9" x 11" pasteboard box whose lid is extravagantly decorated with rich engraving of scrolls, floral bouquets and cherubs centering an engraving of a fashionable woman standing with her three children, a chateau at the background, is labeled in three languages "Season of the Crinoline, a new and rich doll". It contains one paper doll lady, along with eight double-sided (one side blank) crinoline-style costumes and six hats. The costumes are vibrantly colored and enhanced with egg-wash varnish lustre. Four of the costumes feature children at their mother's skirt, with one depicting a young boy and girl holding the box of paper dolls as though beseeching their mother to play with them. The box is marked G.W.F. (block letters) and GWFaber (script). Excellent condition, light box wear. Germany, circa 1860. $4000/5500

Paper Dolls

**38. Collection of Rare Early German Paper Dolls by Josef Scholz**
4.5"-5" uncut dolls. Including a 9.5" x 6" uncut cardboard sheet with 5 paper dolls having variant hair styles and poses (4 girls and 1 boy), along with two additional single uncut dolls, one sheet of uncut hand-colored costumes with matching bonnets, and a large group of matching cut paper dolls and costumes. The sheets are signed "Mainz bei Josef Scholz". Excellent condition. Germany, circa 1860. $800/1000

**39. Large German Paper Lady Doll with Costumes**
10". Heavy pasteboard paper doll with enhancing varnish highlights on hair and costume, self-base, along with 5 double-sided costumes, full-length veil, 2 jackets, face veil, fichu, and three bonnets. The vibrantly colored costumes are enhanced with egg-wash varnish. Excellent condition. Germany, circa 1860. $400/600

**40. Collection of German Uncut Paper Dolls by Josef Scholz**
Including a 9.5" x 6" uncut cardboard sheet with 8 children paper dolls in uncolored costumes along with matching paper sheet of the same costumes, richly colored. And one 13" x 6.5" uncut cardboard sheet with five 5.5" lady paper dolls, uncolored costumes, along with five large sheets of colored costumes, including one sheet of traditional costumes (each is named) and four sheets of fashionable city wear including bonnets. The sheets are signed "Mainz bei Josef Scholz". Excellent condition except 2 largest costume sheets have very ragged edges, and one bonnet is cut from children's costumes. Germany, circa 1860. $800/1100

### 41. *Five Uncut German Paper Doll and Costume Sheets*

12.5" x 9" largest. Comprising a sheet of eight uncut children paper dolls (marked Wenzel, Wissembeg, and Humbert, Paris), sheet of colored costumes for children (marked similarly), cardboard sheet with one paper doll lady, 3 traditional costumes with coiffes and costume elements for coloring, labeled "Poupee L'Anglaise" and "Anzich Puppe", and 2 sheets with exquisite hand-colored double-sided costumes, each sheet with two bonnets, unmarked. Very good condition, light foxing, ragged edges. Germany, circa 1860. $400/500

Paper Dolls

**42. Two French Paper Dolls "Psyche" from Journal de Modes**
9.5". Two heavy cardboard double-sided paper dolls wearing variant lingerie are posed on self bases with label "Psyche, Journal de Modes" on the front and advertising for small boutiques on the reverse base. Included are three double-sided costumes and two bonnets. Excellent condition. France, circa 1860. $400/500

**43. Early French Paper Doll from Journal des Jeunes Personnes with Costumes**
7.5" doll. Heavy cardboard double-sided paper doll is demurely posed on self base labeled "Journal des Jeunes Personnes, Rue Coquillierie 22". Her arms are folded neatly into her torso, allowing a wide variety of arm poses in the 13 double-sided original costumes that are included. Excellent condition, beautifully detailed costumes with strong colors. France, circa 1850's. $500/700

**44. Rare Early Paper Doll and Costumes in Petite Size**
5" doll. Double-sided cardboard doll with head in semi-profile is sturdily constructed with reinforcement bar hidden under lingerie at the back, along with five double-sided hand-colored costumes and 5 bonnets. Excellent condition, one skirt back missing, one costume has unfinished painting at the back. Circa 1840, a rare size with beautiful detail of construction and exquisite minute costume detail. $400/600

**45. French Paper Doll from La Poupee Modele**
8.5" x 6.5". Uncut magazine sheet from the Paris doll journal, features one double-sided paper doll lady, along with one double-sided costume with attached front and back child, and one double-sided bonnet. Labeled "La Poupee Modele, Rue Drouot 2, Paris". Excellent condition, few tiny tears on one side. France, circa 1870. $200/300

**46. French Paper Doll "Psyche" with Costumes and Furniture**
9.5". With one cardboard double-sided paper doll having self base labeled "Psyche, Journal de Modes, Rue Coquilliere" on the front, and advertising for various Parisian boutiques on the reverse of base, along with 4 double-sided costumes. Each of the costumes has an attached piece of furniture (chair, pedestal, piano) allowing the doll to be shown in an interactive environment. Excellent condition. France, circa 1870. $600/900

**47. Very Rare French Boxed Paper Dolls "Les Toilette du Bebe" Along with Uncut Sheet of Same**

6.5" dolls. A heavy pasteboard box, with lithographed cover depicting a scene of 5 children, mother and nanny playing with paper dolls, is labeled "Les Toilettes du Bebe", and contains two double-sided paper dolls, nine double-sided hand-colored costumes, 4 wigs, and five bonnets with wigs in their own miniature decorated box. Several of the costumes feature detail of the child clasping a toy or doll. The cover image is signed B. Collbert (Colibert?), lithographed by Jannin, and published by the premiere French game maker Saussine. Included is a large uncut sheet 19" x 24" of the same set. Excellent condition, bends at doll's necks and ankles, box lid aged. French, circa 1850. $2000/3500

**48. French Paper Dolls and Game Dolls from La Poupee Modele**

Including three 4.5" double-sided paper dolls (one is boy, one is uncut), along with 13 double-sided costumes for the girl (one uncut), and one for the boy. Also included is a miniature booklet "Journal des Poupees" with color engravings, written by Madame Lavalle-Peronne, discussing fashionable costumes for that year's dolls, and six 2" game-piece paper dolls with fashionable costumes. The various pieces were published for and in the French children's journal La Poupee Modele. Very good to excellent condition, one game piece missing head. France, circa 1865. $400/600

# Chapter II. American Paper Dolls 1800-1870

**49. 1840's American Overlay Figures by Scofield & Voorhees**
Four sheets, 4.5" x 7", feature two pairs of overlay paper dolls, one illustrates the "management of pale/dark complexion" by showing judicious use of proper costume colors, and the other, a full-figure model, with die-cut face, compares "simplicity and ornament" in costume. Marked "Scofield & Voorhees, 146 Nassau St". American, 1840's. $300/400

**50. Two Early American Paper Doll Books from Anson Randolph**
Comprising 6" x 7.5" "Paper Doll Furniture: How to Make it" by C.B. Allen with diagrams and patterns for making paper doll furniture, 63 pages; and 4.5" x 7" "Paper Dolls and How to Make Them", new edition improved and enlarged, with 10 original plates, uncut, of various paper dolls and costumes. Both published by Anson Randolph, 1857. Furniture book has water stain throughout, paper doll book has light wear but is intact. American, 1857. $400/600

Paper Dolls

**51. American, Complete Enveloped Sets of "The Paper Doll Family" by Randolph**
Comprising the complete seven piece family set (Father, Mother, Miss Adelaide, Clara, George, The Baby, Bridget the Nurse), each in its own envelope along with complete uncut set of double-sided colored costumes, along with matching uncolored costumes designed for child play. Sizes vary, father is largest at 6.5". Also included is advertising flyer for The Family, and envelope wrap for "Paper Dolls Furniture" with price lists and 8 small furniture accessories. Family is excellent. Anson Randolph, American, circa 1857. $500/800

**52. Two Godey's Lady Book Paper Dolls**
Comprising two sheet's from an 1859 issue of the American lady's fashion magazine, one with colored one-sided costumes, the other page with uncolored dolls designed to wear those costumes. Very good, light spotting, edges rough. American, 1859. $100/200

**53. American Envelope Paper Doll "Mary Lee, The Little Favorite" by Joseph Shaw**
Comprising the uncut paper doll and five-panel folding sheet with five uncut dresses and one hat. Also included is original envelope and sheet "Directions for Cutting Paper Dolls and Dresses". Doll and costumes excellent, envelope worn. Joseph Shaw, Philadelphia, 1850's. $400/700

### 54. American Envelope Paper Dolls "Bessy & Kate" by R.A. Hobbs
Comprising a pair of uncut paper dolls along with a five panel folding sheet with five uncut dresses and one hat, preserved in original envelope with illustration of the doll on the cover. Excellent condition. R.A.Hobbs, Massachusetts, 1850's. $500/700

### 55. American Envelope Paper Doll "Good Two-Shoes" by R.A. Hobbs
Comprising cut doll and uncut six panel folding sheet with five dresses and two hats, preserved in original envelope; also including other original cut elements and some early handmade child's copies. Good to excellent condition. R.A. Hobbs, Massachusetts, 1850's. $500/700

### 56. Rare and Complete 1854 American Boxed Set "Fanny Gray" by Crosby Nichols
A pasteboard box with elaborately scrolled cover design and small image of Fanny Gray in feeding the chickens costume, contains one Fanny head, and five vignette costumes that illustrate various parts of the storyline from the book "Fanny Gray, History of Her Life" (included). Also included is a 6" x 8" background depicting the cottage where Fanny lived. Heavy box wear, neck bend on doll, some spotting, overall good. Published by Crosby, Nichols & Co, printed by S.W. Chandler, Boston, 1854, a rare early and complete American set. $1500/2000

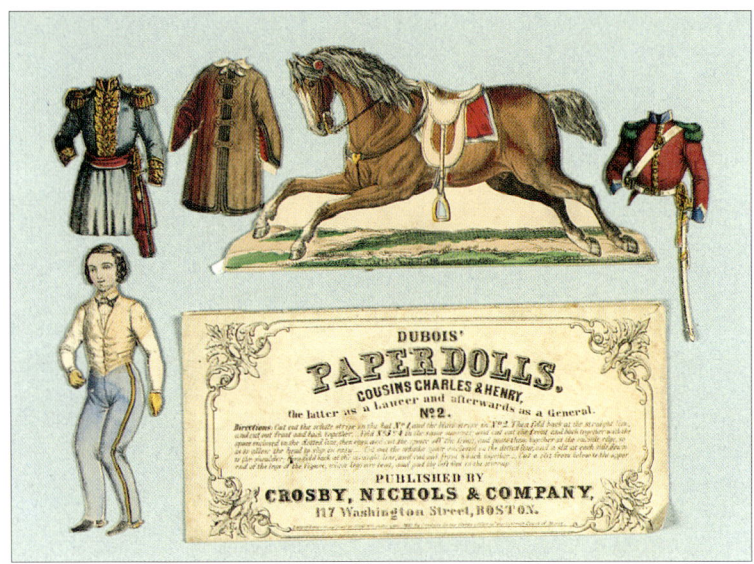

**57. American Envelope Paper Doll "Cousin Charles & Henry" by Crosby Nichols**
4.5". Comprising 1 cut doll with 2 additional cut costumes and a prancing brown horse on platform, within original envelope labeled "Dubois Paper Doll, Cousins Charles & Henry, the latter as a Lancer and afterwards as a General". Very good condition. Published by Crosby, Nichols, of Boston, 1857. $400/600

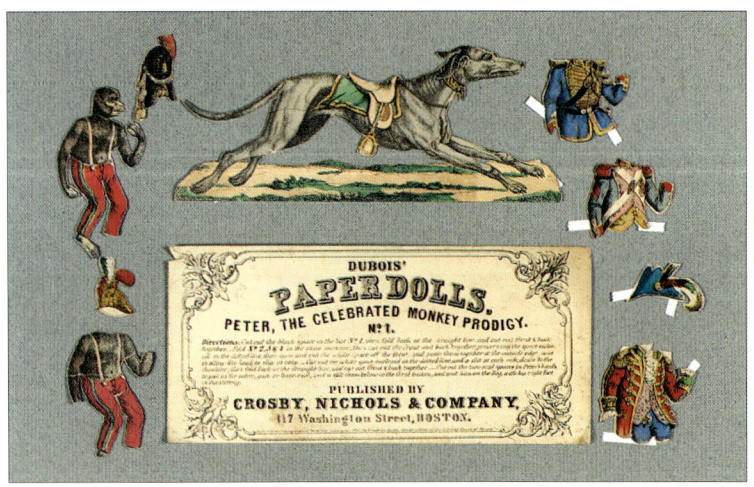

**58. American Envelope Paper Toy "Peter, The Celebrated Monkey Prodigy" by Crosby Nichols**
3". Comprising one cut monkey paper doll with 4 cut costumes and 1 cut hat, along with racing dog for Peter to ride, within original envelope labeled "Dubois Paper Dolls, Peter the Celebrated Monkey Prodigy No1". Very good condition, monkey missing one foot. Published by Crosby, Nichols of Boston, 1857. $400/700

**59. American Paper Doll "Tina Fair" by Degan, Este & Co.**
4.5". Comprising one cut paper doll in original folder with hand-tinted cover, with 5 cut gowns and 2 cut hats. The envelope has inventory list of other available paper dolls on the reverse side. Doll and costumes excellent, cover has light spotting. Published by Degan, Estes & Co, Boston, 1860's. $400/600

**60. American Envelope Paper Doll "Master Frank" by Clark, Austin & Smith**
4". Comprising one cut paper doll and five cut costumes, along with sheet "Directions for Master Frank" and the original envelope "The Girls' Delight, Paper Dolls Number Three, Master Frank" with an inventory of the costumes included within. Excellent condition. Published by Clark, Austin & Smith, of New York, 1858. $300/400

**61. American Envelope Paper Doll "Nellie, a Young Lady of the Upper Ten" by Clark, Austin & Smith**
5.5". Comprising one cut paper doll of woman with gloved hands and fan, 5 cut costumes, 5 cut bonnets, and a large sheet with pattern and directions for making more costumes, and advertising for other paper dolls on the reverse, in original envelope labeled "The Girls' Delight Paper Dolls Number 4, Nellie- a young lady of the 'upper ten' with dresses &c sufficient in number and elegance for a princess of 'the blood'". Excellent condition. Published by Clark, Austin & Smith of New York, 1858. $400/600

Paper Dolls

**62. American Paper Doll "My Dear Papa" by Chromatic Printing**
2.5" doll. A small folding booklet, 3" x 2", entitled "My Dear Papa" features an uncut gentleman paper doll along with three uncut costumes and hats. Included is advertising for other "penny books" by that firm, and cover for "Our Little Peggie". Excellent condition, except separation on fold-out, slight age darkening. Philadelphia, circa 1875. $200/400

**63. American Paper Doll "Sallie" by Peter Thomson**
4" doll. An uncut fold-out booklet features one doll and three costumes with matching hats. The booklet cover shows "Sallie" in a 4th costume, holding a doll. Marked "Peter G. Thomson, Cincinnati". Fine condition. Circa 1880. $300/400

**64. American Paper Doll "Louise" by Peter Thomson**
4" doll. An uncut fold-out booklet features one doll and three costumes with matching hats. The booklet cover depicts "Louise" in another costume holding a racquet. Marked "Peter G. Thomson, Cincinnati". Fine condition. Circa 1880. $300/400

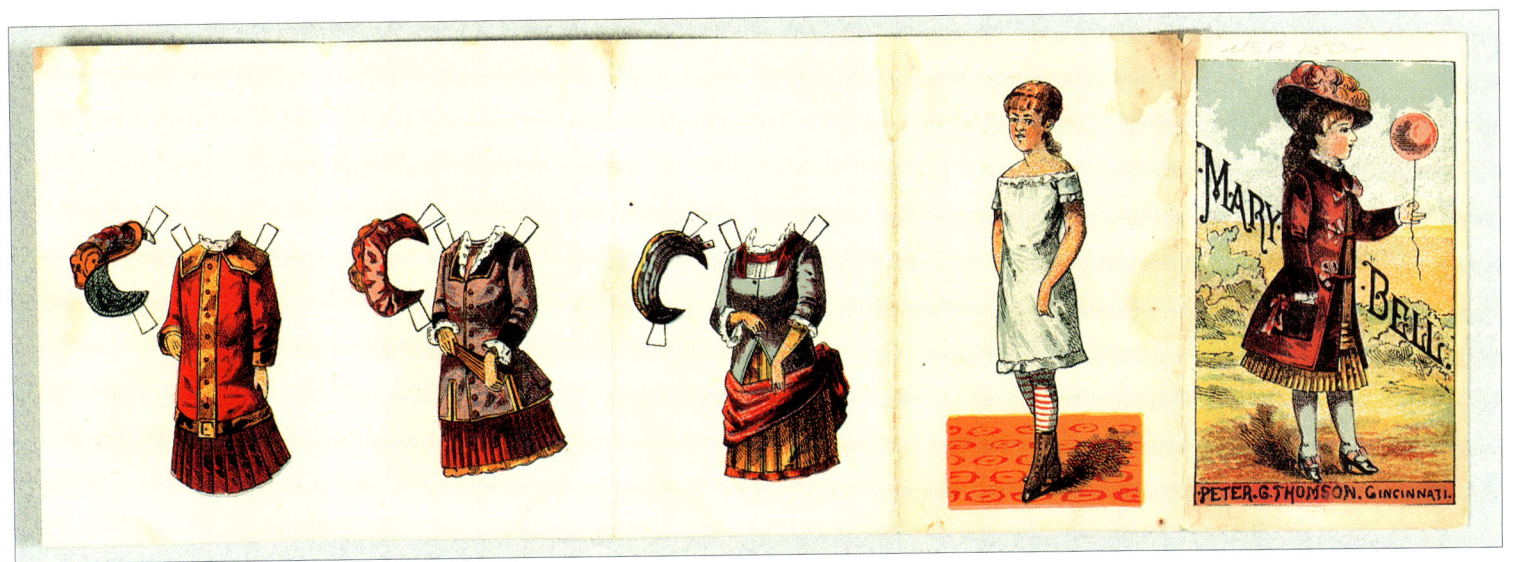

### 65. American Paper Doll "Rhoda" by Peter Thomson
4" doll. An uncut fold-out booklet features one doll and three costumes with matching hats. The booklet cover depicts "Rhoda" in one other costume. Marked "Peter G. Thomson, Cincinnati". Also included is a children's book "The Seven Ravens" published by Thomson. Fine condition. Circa 1880. $300/400

### 66. American Paper Doll "Mary Bell" by Peter Thomson
4" doll. An uncut fold-out booklet features one doll and three costumes with matching hats. The booklet cover depicts "Mary Beth" in profile view, holding balloon. Marked "Peter G. Thomson, Cincinnati". Excellent condition, some spotting. Circa 1880. $200/300

### 67. American Paper Doll "Little Bo Peep" by McLoughlin
4.5" doll. A cut paper doll clasping a lamb, along with three additional one-side costumes, and the original booklet cover. Marked McLoughlin Bros, New York. Excellent condition. Circa 1880. $200/250

Paper Dolls

### 68. *American Rare and Beautiful Paper Doll and Costume Sheets from Frank Leslie's Lady Magazine*

5.5" doll. Two 11.5" x 8" uncut sheets from the lady's monthly magazine feature one double-sided doll with base, and five double-sided costumes. One costume is notable for having additional matching cape, and there are also 7 hair-pieces or hats with attached hair. Marked "Paper Dolls, chromolithographed expressly for Frank Leslie's Lady Magazine, The Major & Knapp Eng Mfg & Litho Co, 449 Broadway, NY. Circa 1866. $300/400

### 69. *Two American Overlays from Miss Leslie's Magazine*

9.5" x 6" pages. Four pages (2 sets) of overlays along with printed page from 1843 Miss Leslie's Magazine; one pair of overlays with color tinted detail of costume, the other pair uncolored and labeled "The Rustic Maid" or "The City Belle". Very good uncut condition, light foxing. American, 1843. $200/300

### 70. *Two American Walking Paper Dolls by Hart*
5.5" assembled. Component paper dolls with beautifully lithographed features of face, hair and costume feature separate lower torso with legs, and upper torso with head. Skirts are designed to attach the two pieces, and by swinging the skirt to and fro give an appearance of "walking" to the doll. Also included is one extra child's head. The skirts are marked "Dresses in great variety sold separately, patented Dec.1, 1874. Attributed to Hart, America, 1874. Very good condition. $200/250

### 71. *American Handmade Paper Doll of Marie Antoinette*
6" doll. Hand-drawn, colored and cut one-side paper doll and costumes features a lady in the manner of late 18th century, along with 8 gowns and 6 hats made by the same hand, each with exquisite soft colors enhanced by intricate detail of workmanship. The set is included in an early box with paper-lace edged interior, along with envelope ink-script labeled "Marie Antoinette paper dolls, costumes copies from portraits and paintings". Doll and costumes excellent, box worn. American, age uncertain but probably late 19th century. $800/1200

Paper Dolls

**72. American Paper Doll "Ida Mae" by McLoughlin**
8". Cardboard cut-out double-sided paper doll of young lady with green rosette ribbons in hair, on self base, along with four double-sided cut-out gowns. Very good condition, slight bends at neck and ankles. McLoughlin, circa 1860. $200/400

**73. American Paper doll "Ella Hall" by McLoughlin**
4.5" doll. A booklet with colored cover includes an uncut paper doll labeled "Ella Hall" along with four uncut costumes and one bonnet. The inside front cover includes Directions for Making, and the outer cover is marked "McLoughlin Bros, New York". Excellent condition. Circa 1860. $200/250

**74. American Paper Doll "Lilly Beers" by McLoughlin**
4" doll. A booklet cover with image of the paper doll is labeled "McLouglin Bros, Manufacturers, New York" and contains one cut paper doll and five cut costumes. Excellent condition. Circa 1860. $150/200

**75. Two American Paper Dolls "Groom" and "Grooms-man" by McLoughlin**
8.5" dolls. Comprising two double-sided paper doll gentlemen in formal wear, one with moustache, along with six double-sided costumes, and one top hat. Excellent condition. American, 1875. $200/300

Paper Dolls

# Chapter III. 1880-WWI Era

**76. Pair, German Mr. and Mrs. Bunny Paper Dolls by Wezel & Naumann**
10.5" dolls. Posed standing, the bunnies each have 3 costumes with colorful Springtime themes, along with three hats that fit over their ears and three pairs of shoes. Each costume and bunny is signed on reverse "Wezel & Naumann, Leipzig", printed by Druck lithographers. Excellent condition, Mr. Bunny's ears are reinforced. Germany, circa 1910. $300/500

**77. German, Large Collection of Cut and Uncut Paper Dolls**
Comprising two 7" x 8" uncut sheets with single-side lady paper doll and extensive gowns and accessories; one 8" x 6" uncut sheet with double-sided boy and girl dolls with costumes and accessories, mark J.S.; another similar sheet partially cut with one doll and costumes; and a large group of cut paper dolls and costumes, by the same maker. Excellent condition. Germany, circa 1890. $300/400

Paper Dolls

**78. German, Collection of Embossed Paper Dolls of the Royal Family**
6" largest. Included are Kaiserine Victoria Augusta, Prince Von Prenken – King of Prussia, Prince Adelbert, Princes August Wilhelm, three other children, and a baby, along with a large collection of costumes for each, including fashionable lady's wear, military uniforms, classic children's costumes. Although played with, the dolls and costumes remain fresh and vibrant, 2 children with neck repairs. Germany, circa 1884. $400/500

### 79. German, Two Uncut Sheets of "German National Costumes"

9" x 14". Heavy paper uncut sheets each feature one double-sided paper doll (one man, one woman), along with four traditional folklore style costumes and various accessories. The man is wearing costumes of "environs of Hamburg" and the woman wears costumes of "Black Forest". Attached is the original label (in English) "#62, National Costumes of Germany". Marked JS (intertwined) 62. Excellent condition, few ragged corners. Germany, circa 1890. $200/300

### 80. German, Two Embossed Uncut Paper Doll Sheets

12" x 14" sheets. Each large sheet has uncut paper dolls and costumes, each in rich vibrant colors with superb details of accessories or ephemera. Sheet #839 features two women, boy and girl; a second unnumbered sheet features two fashionable ladies. Each marked W&S. Excellent condition, 839 has scissors cut but no missing pieces. Germany, circa 1890. $300/400

### 81. Set, German Embossed Paper Dolls in Original Box

4". A heavy pasteboard box with blue paper cover and chromolithograph on the lid depicting two children at play includes three embossed varnished paper dolls and six colorful embossed costumes each with attached bonnet, and 2 other bonnets. Excellent condition. Germany, circa 1890. $200/300

**82. French Lady Paper Doll from the Turn-of-the-19th-Century**
10.5". An embossed cardboard doll depicting a slender elegant lady from the end of the 19th century has self base and easel back, along with two embossed gowns (one with matching bonnet) and one embossed coat trimmed with ermine and having matching cap and muff. Doll is marked 74333. Excellent condition. French, circa 1900. $200/300

**83. French Embossed Girl with Fanciful Costumes**
8". An embossed cardboard doll depicting a young lady with long curly locks had Tuck-style neck and easel back, and owns four elaborately designed gowns with rich accessories such as jewelry, boa feather fan, or basket. Excellent condition, neck glued. French, circa 1895. $250/350

**84. German Paper Doll Portraying Prince Edward of Wales**
5.5" Historical paper doll portraying the popular English Prince Edward of Wales, along with three additional costumes including hunting costume. Excellent condition. Germany, circa 1900. $100/150

**85. Large Group of German Articulated Paper Dolls by L&B & Others**
5"- 14". Each is cardboard figure with grommet-jointed arms and legs to allowing infinite articulation, and having embossed detailing with richly painted and highlighted details. The group includes two large ballerinas, three large ladies (one, #2686, still unassembled, and one missing arms and one leg), 2 medium ballerinas, 1 medium, lady, 2 small ladies, 1 black baby, 1 Dennison baby, and three children (one with 6 handmade costumes). Mostly German, circa 1900. $400/500

### 86. Four Uncut Sheets "Poupees a Habiller" by Pellerin D'Epinal

10.5" x 14.5" Each is a heavy paper sheet with front and back images of one child and 4 front and back costumes along with generous accessories. The costumes range from daily fashionable costumes to fanciful fairy tale wear. Marked "Imagerie D'Epinal, Imagerie Pellerin, Poupees a Habiller, Genre Superieur", and include Plates 1-4. Excellent condition. French, end of 19th century. $300/400

### 87. French Uncut Sheet by Imageries Reunies Janville-Nancy

7" x 11". An uncut sheet printed on both sides features 3 paper dolls (2 women and 1 man) along with six fold-over costumes and ases. Two costumes feature Pierrot and Harlequin theater designs. Marked "Personnages et Poupees a Habiller (recto-verso), Imagerie-Reunies, Jarville-Nancy". Excellent condition, tape stains at corners. French, end of 19th century. $100/150

**88. French, *Four Uncut Sheets of Paper Dolls***
16" x 12" largest. Each is uncut heavy paper sheet featuring front and back paper dolls with a wide myriad of costumes in rich detail. Included are pair of Costumes Etrangers shown at the Exposition of 1900 (#1122, 1121), and Petit Costumier (1066, 1065). All by Pellerin & Cie, Imagerie D'Epinal. Excellent condition. French, end of 19th century. $300/400

**89. *Seven Articulated Dancing Dolls and Uncut Polichinelle Postcard***
8"-14". Includes 5 heavy cardboard figures with hand-colored detail (one identical on back as Lord Dundreary, probably English) and two larger French Polichinelle and Harlequin, each with loosely articulated hips and knees (the French with additional jointing at shoulders). Along with Pellerin postcard, #1340, depicting Polichinelle Pantin. Excellent condition, one English model missing one lower leg. Late 19th century. $300/400

Paper Dolls

**90. German Uncut Sheet "Aschenbrodel" by Druck**
14" x 17". A large uncut sheet depicting one single-sided 9" paper doll girl, along with four fairytale costumes and many accessories to complete the fairy tale imagery. Marked "No 108 glatt, No 109 gepragt., Druck und Verlag Hohenstein & Lange, Berlin-Deponiert", and stamped "Aschenbrodel". Excellent condition except some ragged side edges. Germany, circa 1890. $200/300

**91. German Paper Doll "Liesel und Sein Schwesterchen"**
9.5". An embossed paper doll with easel back, Tuck-style neck, owns two costumes and two bonnets. Included is (very worn) original box indicating name of set, the fact that it originally included two paperdolls, model number 59208 and WH initials. Doll and costumes excellent with vibrant colors. Germany, late 19th century. $200/300

**92. Rare French Boxed Set of Paper Dolls "Sleeping Beauty"**
7.5". A cardboard box wih cover illustration depicting Prince Charming awakening Sleeping Beauty is labeled "La Belle au Bois Dormant et le Prince Charmant, Depose 74350", and includes three embossed easel back paper dolls with Tuck style neck attachment along with 3 gowns for Sleeping Beauty, 4 jackets and 1 suit of armor for Prince, sleeping Beauty's bed, drum, dog, and 10 hats or head pieces. Box is very worn, contents excellent with rich detailing of costumes, colors and embossing. French, late 19th century. $300/500

**93. English "Bonnie Billie" From Our Bonnie Series by Raphael Tuck**
9". Cardboard figure of young brown-haired boy with easel back, along with four tabbed costumes, each featuring a little toy, and one hat. Marked "Bonnie Billie #65, Copyright by Raphael Tuck, Designed at The Studios in New York". Excellent condition. Circa 1920. $200/300

**94. English "Bonnie Babbie" From Our Bonnie Series by Raphael Tuck**
9". Cardboard figure of young girl with four tabbed costumes and four bonnets. Marked "Bonnie Babbie #67, Copyright by Raphael Tuck, Designed at The Studios in New York". Excellent condition except easel back missing and some backside pencil scribbles on girl. Circa 1920. $200/300

**95. English "Little Martha" from Colonial Belles Series by Raphael Tuck**
9". Cardboard figure of young girl with white hair in the colonial fashion along with 4 tabbed colonial style costumes and four matching bonnets. Costumes excellent, doll has neck bend and right front foot missing. Marked "Raphael Tuck Artistic Seris #750". Circa 1900. $150/250

Paper Dolls

**96. English "Bonnie Betty" from Our Bonnie Series by Raphael Tuck**
9". Cardboard figure of young girl with short curly brown hair, along with 4 tabbed costumes, each with attached accessory. Marked "Bonnie Betty #66, Copyright by Raphael Tuck, Designed at The Studios in New York". Excellent condition, easel back missing. Circa 1920. $200/300

**97. English "Miss Julia Marlowe" from Famous Faces Series by Raphael Tuck**
9.5". Cardboard figure of adult woman with easel back and neck slit owns four costumes depicting her character is her famous theatrical roles, including Constance in "Love Chase", Rosalind in "As You Like It", "Barbara Frietchie", and "Colinette". Marked "Miss Julia Marlowe, Raphael Tuck, US Patent November 20, 1894. Included is (broken) lid of original box. Excellent condition. Circa 1895. $400/500

**98. English "Happy Harold" from Our Playmates Series by Raphael Tuck**
10", Cardboard figure of young boy with curly brown hair, easel back and neck slit, having four costumes and two hats. Marked "Raphael Tuck, Pat. Nov 20, 1894". Along with original box indicating model #45. Excellent condition. Circa 1895. $300/400

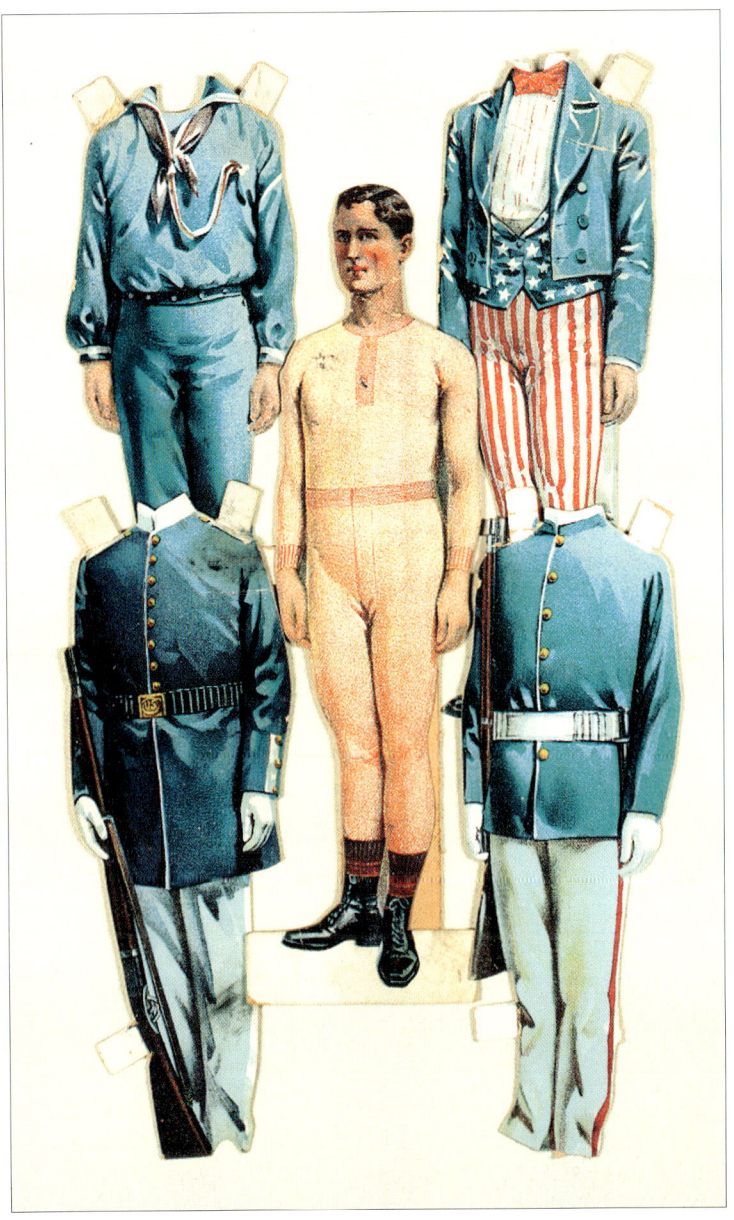

**99. English "Our Little Treasure" from Raphael Tuck**
12". Cardboard figure of young girl holding a doll, easel back and slit neck, having six costumes each with detailed accessories ranging from a dog to a Bible to a wedding gown with bridal bouquet, along with two bonnets. Marked Raphael Tuck. Excellent condition. Circa 1895. $300/500

**100. English "Under The Stars and Stripes" from New Series by Raphael Tuck**
7.5" Cardboard figure of adult man in one piece knit undergarments, easel back, along with four tabbed military or patriotic costumes including Uncle Sam. Worn original envelope is also included. Good condition, moderate wear. Raphael Tuck. Circa 1895. $400/500

Paper Dolls

**101. English Wedding Party Paper Dolls by Raphael Tuck**
9.5". Includes groom with slit neck, easel back, four costumes and one hat, Artistic Series 401A; Bride with slit neck, 4 costumes and 1 partial hat, Artistic Series #600; and Bridesmaid, with slit neck, easel back, 4 costumes includes bicyclist and dress with attached dog at base, 4 bonnets, Artistic Series 503. Very good/excellent condition. Bridesmaid especially fine. Circa 1895.
$400/500

***102. English "Sunny Susan" from Little Maids Series by Raphael Tuck***
13". Cardboard figure of young girl with brown curly hair and topknot, slit neck, along with two costumed and three bonnets. Marked Raphael Tuck, with 1895 date. Excellent condition, left hand bent, easel back missing. Circa 1895. $200/300

***103. English Paper Doll, Unnamed, by Raphael Tuck***
13". Cardboard figure of young girl with flowing light brown hair and having permanent costume of colorful undergarments, holding a hair brush, slit neck. Along with three additional costumes including one holding a doll. Marked Raphael Tuck. Excellent condition, slight neck bend, right ankle bend, easel back missing. Circa 1895. $300/400

***104. English Paper Doll "Young American" by Raphael Tuck***
6.5" Cardboard paper doll of young boy in blue union suit and leggings, along with 3 additional costumes. Marked "Young America, Artistic Series #4, Designed at The Studios in New York, Printed in Bavaria". The set was originally presented in a paper doll trunk in this series (not included). Very good condition, one foot repaired. Circa 1895. $200/300

Paper Dolls

**105. Three Sets, English Paper Dolls from Belle Series by Tuck**
9" dolls. Each paper doll depicting an adult woman, slit neck, easel back, including Belle of the South with 4 costumes, 2 hats; Belle of Saratoga with 4 costumes, 2 hats, and original wrapper; and Belle of the West with 4 costumes, 1 hat and original wrapper. Very good to excellent condition. Circa 1895. $300/500

**106. English Die-cut Scraps of Royal Kings by Raphael Tuck**
6". Seven die-cut figures with embossed and glazed detail feature seven English kings of the Middle Ages each wearing royal robes. Tuck, circa 1890. Very good/excellent condition. $150/200

**107. English, Six Articulated Paper Animals by Raphael Tuck**
10"l. tiger. Each is of heavy cardboard with richly embossed detailing, and features articulation of the neck and limbs. Each has information about the animal printed on the reverse side and Raphael Tuck indicia. Included are lion, tiger, tiger pair, bear pair, rhinoceros, and lioness. Excellent condition. Tuck. Circa 1910. $200/300

Paper Dolls

**108. English Paper Doll "Domestic Pets" from Dressing Dolls Series by Tuck**
6.5". Cardboard paper doll of young girl with unusual detail of loosely attached long braid of hair, slit neck, along with 1 additional costume featuring the girl holding a baby lamb, two bonnets, 2 pairs of shoes, 2 un-paired shoes. From the New Series of Dressing Dolls, #33 by Raphael Tuck, circa 1895. Excellent condition. $200/300

**109. German Embossed Figural Santa's and Christmas Tree with "Surprise" Paper Dolls**
6" closed. Three die-cut embossed figures include two of traditional St. Nicholas (one blue-suited, one red-suited) and decorated Christmas tree. Each folds open to reveal a die-cut paper doll along with various costumes and die-cut toys and teddies. Excellent condition. Germany, circa 1890. $700/900

Paper Dolls

**110. English Paper Doll Book "Dolly Darling and Her Pretty Clothes" by Ernest Nister**
9" x 10". A hardbound book with vibrantly chromolithographed cover depicting two children playing with a paper doll features 11 uncut interior pages of paper dolls, each with 2 costumes and accessories (6 are color lithographed, 5 are line drawings designed for a child to color (2 missing pages are Japanese and Fritz). Excellent condition, 2 missing paper dolls (Japanese and Fritz), one page loose. Ernest Nister, London, New York, model 2739, illustrated by E. Heatly. Inscribed in ink on inside cover "Virginia, Christmas 1917". $300/400

**111. English Boxed Paper Doll "Daisy and Her Dresses" by Spears**
11" x 9.5" box. 10" doll. The box with delicately painted paper doll and costume on the lid contains two paper doll bodies (one labeled "Daisy", one labeled "Spear's Original Character Doll #5484" and four interchangeable heads, all with embossed and varnished details. Along with 5 dresses and 3 bonnets. Box is marked "Designed in England, Spear's Series Registered, J.W.S & S Bavaria". Box repaired with archival tape, head reinforcement on dolls, overall very good/excellent. England, circa 1910. $400/600

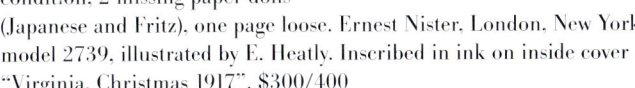

## The Up-To-Date Dollies.

These Dollies come to meet you here,
Both most attractive, that is clear;
The newest fashions they each wear,
One bonny boy, one maiden fair.

You soon will learn what they can do,
By reading these nice verses through;
You'll be surprised the fun they make,
When you a little trouble take.

To make them stand, take Dolly's head
'Twixt thumb and finger of right hand;
Then with the left hand part the feet,
When balanced, it will look so sweet.

But if at first you try in vain,
Your best plan is to try again;
Don't get impatient, just be kind,
And how to do it, soon you'll find.

They'll stand up, sit down, kneel, or fight,
When you have learnt to place them right;
Bow heads, shake hands, and jump-backs play,
Do everything but run away.

Now see them in their big new car,
They'll go away to — oh! so far;
Then back they'll come, and you can now,
Dress them up again, I'll vow.

They undress too — if you with care
Lift up their arms, their hands in air;
Then pull off sleeves — unfasten gown
Or coat in front — don't fear they'll frown.

Pull gently till the collar's free
From Dolly's arms — You'll quickly see;
And when you'd dress them both again,
Reverse these movements — that's quite plain.

Then you, if you a prank enjoy,
Can dress a girl up as a boy;
On Jennie's head put Bobby's hat,
All sorts of funny things like that.

Remember this, if you are kind,
Good children they will be, you'll find;
And never one of them refuse,
Your hours of play - time to amuse.

Then when the clock strikes, six, seven, eight,
And nurse comes in and says 'tis late;
Put them to bed upon the shelf,
Before you go to bed yourself.

Uncle Clifton.

**112. English Boxed Paper Dolls "Dollies Up-to-Date" by Misch & Co**
8" x 13" box. 12" dolls. A cardboard box with interior flaps containing a poem about the dolls, costumes and cards, contains a dimensional pop-out open-top double-sided automobile with movable wheels, double-side boy and girl paper dolls with articulation of neck, shoulders, waist, hips, and knees, 3 costumes and 1 sailor cap for boy, four hats and parasol for girl, toot-toot auto horn, and pair of auto headlights. The articulation of the dolls allows them to sit inside the car, to or stand. The box is marked "Misch & Co. London. Designed in England. Printed in Germany". Box very worn, contents very good to excellent, with some play wear and bends. England, circa 1910. $400/600

DOLLY'S WARDROBE,

DIRECTIONS FOR USE.

Place the double head through the slit in the centre of the double skirts, and when half way through give it a half turn. Stand the double skirt up and the head will then rest upon the top of the same. Now start putting on the bodices which are easily adjusted by placing the loop at the back of each bodice over the flange which is eyeletted to the body. As soon as you have dressed one side, you can turn it round and dress the other side in a like manner. With each box of Dolly's Wardrobe a bodice, or blouse, will be found to match each skirt, as also the hats, which are not stuck together on the under side, and so can be fitted on to the heads. When you have finished dressing the two dolls that you started with, take off the bodices and hats, catch hold of the head which is hanging down inside the two skirts, and reverse the latter, when you will have two more dolls to dress. Presuming that you have dressed the four long skirts, take out the heads, and place them in the same way as described above into the short skirts, when the same process can be gone through with these.

Very great amusement can also be obtained, and some very charming costumes made, by trying on the bodices belonging, strictly speaking, to other costumes upon the various skirts, and in this way 144 changes can be effected.

LONDON.
DEAN & SON, LTD.,
160A, FLEET ST., E.C.

W&Co. TRADE MARK
WOLF & Co.,
PHILADELPHIA, NEW YORK,
AND CHICAGO

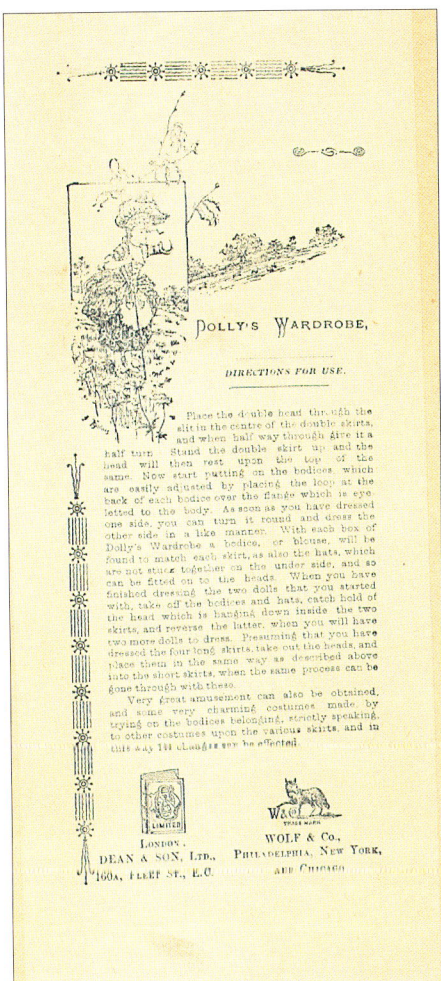

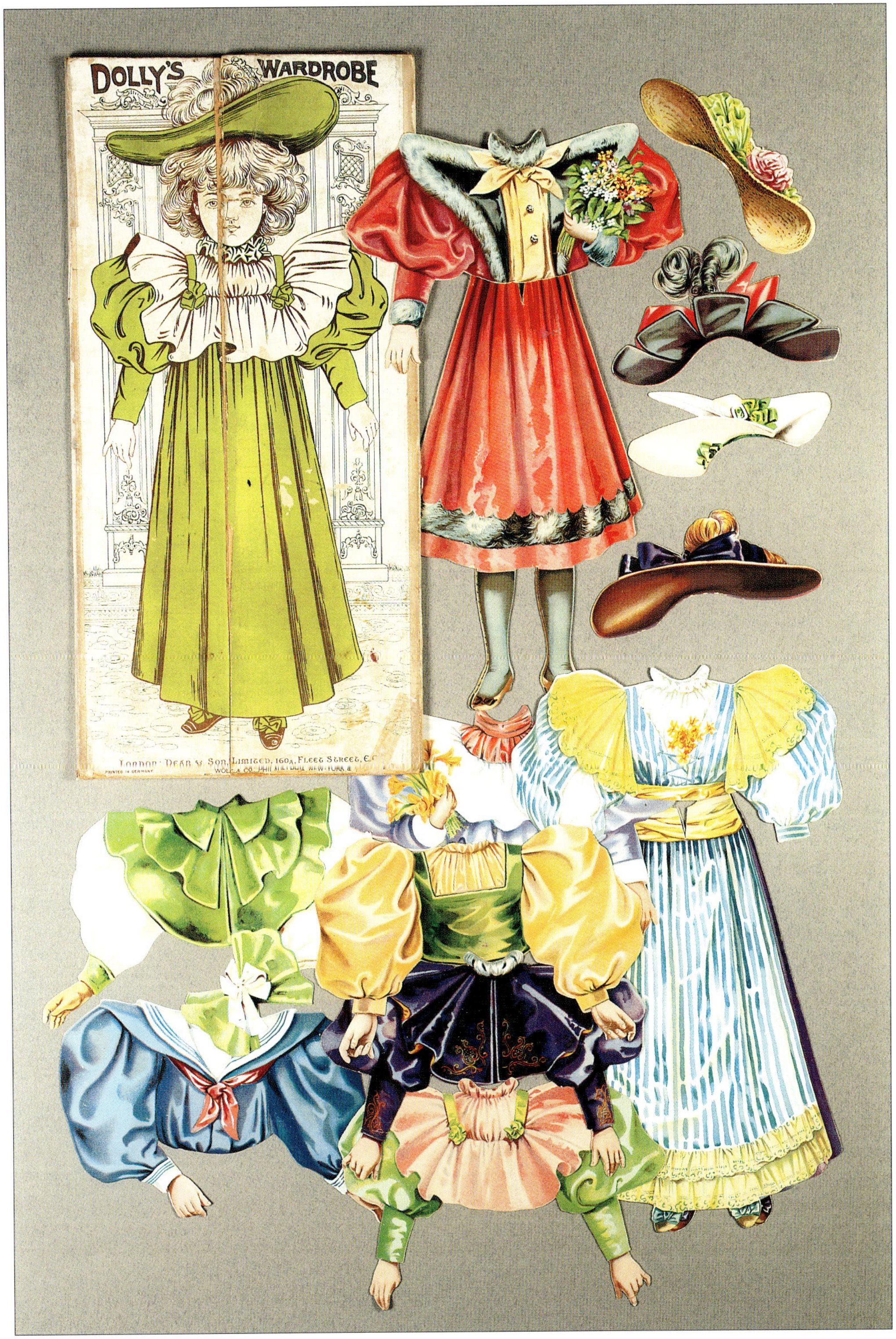

***113. English Large Folio Set "Dolly's Wardrobe" by Dean & Co.***
9" x 17" folio. 16" doll assembled. Two double-sided attached doll heads have alternate faces and hair on either side (4 faces). The costumes are designed to hide the faces not in play. Included are 8 single-sided blouses, 4 double-sided bonnets (different on each side), and 2 double-sided and flip-over skirts of alternate lengths (thus, 8 different skirts). The interior folio flaps include instructions for play including the idea of mix and matching blouses and skirts, proclaiming that a total of 144 different looks could be achieved. Marked " Dean & Co, Limited, 160a Fleet Street, London, Wolf & Co, Philadelphia, Printed in Germany". Folio worn, contents excellent with vivid coloring. England, circa 1895. $600/900

**114. English Boxed Paper Dolls "Dolly with Interchangeable Heads" by Spears**
8" x 8" box. 10" dolls. Cardboard box contains one heavy cardboard doll body with embossed details and rich varnished colors, 4 interchangeable heads of young child, 3 costumes, 4 bonnets, and 3 accessory playthings including a doll. Box worn with lid design missing, dolls and contents excellent except replaced neck dowel on body (hidden when assembled). England, Spears, circa 1920. $200/300

**115. English Boxed Paper Dolls "Dolly Dear" by Spears**
6" 12" box. 10" doll. Contained in original box with colorful cover is a set with six interchangeable heads and one body, is of heavy cardboard with embossed varnished detail, and includes 4 single-sided embossed dresses, 3 bonnets, feathered wrap, tambourine, purse, and teddy bear. The heads are printed with different name on the reverse of each: Agnes, Edith, Fanny, Irene, Emmy and Alice, and can be interchanged by slipping over the neck dowel of the body. Marked "Spear's Patent Character Dolls with changeable heads". England, Spears, circa 1910. $500/800

**116. Boxed Paper Dolls "Nouvelles Poupees a Habiller" for the French Market**
8" x 9" box. 6.5" & 5.5" dolls. A cardboard box with cover image depicting a young boy and girl in refined clothing is titled in both French and Dutch, and contains boy and girl paper dolls with chest tab for holding 5 costumes and 4 bonnets for the girl, 4 costumes and 3 hats for the boy, and six accessories or toys including doll, teddy, pull toys and ball. Marked "JSM No. 122". Dolls and costumes excellent, girl has neck reinforcement, light box bear. Circa 1910. $300/500

**117. German Boxed Paper Dolls "Bruderlein & Schwesterlein, Frere & Soeur"**
6" x 10" box. 8" –8.5" dolls. A cardbord box with decorations in the Art Nouveau style depicts a teen-age brother and sisters and is labeled in both German and French. Inside are 2 single-sided easel back paper dolls, boy with 5 costumes, and girl with 6 costumes. Marked "No80" on box lid. Excellent condition of box, dolls and costumes. Germany, circa 1910. $500/800

Paper Dolls

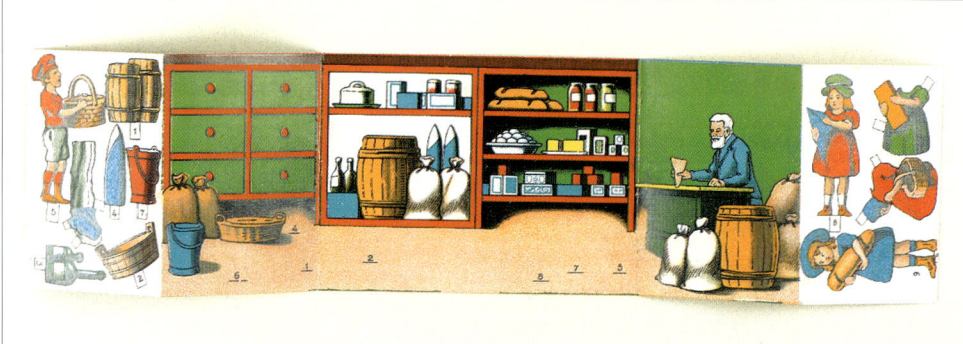

### 119. German "My Smallest Doll's Room" with Paper Doll
3" x 14" unfolded. 2" paper doll. A folding five-panel sheet features three-folded of a grocery store scene with indications of where the three paper dolls should be placed. Each doll has 1 extra costume and there are 3 acccessories. Excellent, uncut, in original envelope stamped Germany No.10303. Circ 1920. $50/100

### 118. English "Dolly's Wardrobe" Boxed Paper Doll Set by Spears
12" x 6" box. 10" dolls. An outer box with raised gilded script lettering "Dolly's Wardrobe" contains a dimensional paper armoire with opening door and drawer and gilded metal clasps, two easel back single-side paper dolls with embossed varnished details, and an extensive trousseau with embossed and varnished detail: 8 dresses designed to hang on wire frames inside the armoire, 8 bonnets, and 6 accessories including feather stole, fan, purses, teddy and fur muff. The dolls are each marked with their name "Daisy" & "Dorothy" and Spears. Armoire, costumes and Dorothy excellent, box a bit worn, Daisy has neck and one arm tape. England, Spears, circa 1910. $700/900

**120. German Miniature Folio "Doll Sheets for Little Girls"**
4" doll. 3.5" x 4.5" folio. A paper folio cover with elegant lettering contains two fold-out panels, each with three uncut sheets that contain double-sided embossed doll, six-double-sided costumes three pinafores, and a myriad of double-sided accessories from bonnets to tennis racquet to watering can. Booklet is marked W&SB No.174. Made in Germany. Excellent condition. Germany, circa 1895. $150/250

**121. Three Uncut Sheets "Fashion Dolls Series"**
8" x 5.5" sheet. Each cardboard sheet includes one doll and two costumes with matching accessories. The original paper wrapper is labeled "Fashion Dolls Series, Sold Assorted Only, Three Designs". Excellent condition. Circa 1910. $100/150

**122. American Envelope Paper Dolls "Tiny Ladies" and "Tiny Tots"**
9" and 5.5". In their original envelopes are three single-sided easel back paper dolls, the 2 larger dolls each with 3 dresses and 2 or 3 bonnets, and the small boy with one jacket. One costume features her hands clasping an envelope addressed to "Miss Love, Heart St. USA". Dolls and costumes excellent. Envelopes worn. Circa 1900. $200/300

Paper Dolls

**123. Four American Paper Dolls by Selchow and Richter**
8.5" dolls. Each is single-sided cardboard doll with easel back, including "Dolly with 3 costumes and 3 hats; "Lady Belle" with 1 costume and envelope; "Flossie" with 1 dess and 2 hats; and Little Laddie with envelope, 3 costumes and 2 hats. Good/very good condition, envelopes very worn, some bends. Selchow and Richter, circa 1900. $200/300

**124. American Paper Dolls "American Beauty"**
9" dolls. Includes two single-sided easel back paper dolls, along with 5 hats and 6 costumes (one holding a doll). Maker unknown, identical dolls have been found with Owens Famous Bread advertising and the dolls also are identical to the Rosebud Series. Very good condition. American, circa 1900. $100/150

**125. American Paper Doll Book "The New Model Book of Dolls"**
A beautifully lithographed book with vibrant cover depicting a girl playing with paper dolls (while her cat on the floor is destroying one!) contains uncut pages of well-detailed doll costumes and accessories. Excellent condition, some slight ragged edges on cover. McLoughlin, circa 1895. $200/300

**126. American Paper Doll Book "Nursery Rhyme Party Dolls in Costume" by McLoughlin**
10" x 13" book. 10.5" dolls. Included are two punch-out paper dolls on back cardboard cover, and six uncut pages of identified nursery rhyme paper doll costumes. The beautifully illustrated cover features the "Queen of Hearts". Marked McLoughlin Bros. American, circa 1900. Excellent condition. $100/200

Paper Dolls

**127. American Paper Dolls "Teddy Bear" and "Chanticleer" by Ottmann**

10.5" bear. Including teddy bear paper doll, single-sided with easel back, having five single-sided costumes including vintage baseball uniform, 2 hats and original envelope labeled "Published by J. Ottmann Litho Co, NY". Along with Chanticleer girl paper doll with two dresses. Excellent except bear envelope very worn, girl missing foot. Ottmann, circa 1910. $200/300

**128. American Celebrity Paper Doll "Miss Kate Castledon"**

5.5" doll. Featuring uncut double-sided paper doll with four sheets of uncut dresses and hats, in original envelope with image of the actress and title "The Idol of the Fun Loving Public, Miss Kate Castledon". Excellent condition. American, Forbes Co, circa 1885. $200/300

*Historical note: The popular late-19th century American actress and songwriter ("Oh George, Get Out of the Way", was one notable work) performed in small town and big city theatres, and was notorious for traveling with her $1000 dog. She died in 1892.*

Paper Dolls

**129. Two American Paper Dolls by Dutton**
Includes 10" "Little Red Riding Hood", single-sided with easel back, and 3 costumes with 3 bonnets, original envelope; and 9" brunette side-sided easel back girl from "Fairy Tales" with 7 gowns. Envelope labeled "Dutton's Dolls for Dressing" London Ernest Nister, New York Dutton & Co, Printed in Bavaria 1311". Excellent condition, few bends. Circa 1900. $150/200

**130. American Paper Doll Book "Little Faces from Far Places"**
9" x 12". The hardbound book, illustrated and written by Julia Nordell, features seven full page illustrations of paper dolls and costumes from Joanna's adventures in European travel. Copyright 1933. Very good condition, wear on cover edges, all paper dolls uncut. American, published by Grosset & Dunlap. $100/150

**131. American Miniature Paper Doll Book "The Unhappy Paper Doll"**
5" x 4". Written by Josephine Lawrence, illustrated by Joseph Claghorn, published by Barse & Co of New York and Newark. Features the stories of Miss Bella, a paper doll. Excellent condition. Copyright 1928. $100/200

**132. American Boxed Paper Dolls "Famous Queens and Martha Washington" by E.S. Tucker**

10" x 8" box. The completely uncut set features seven paper dolls of famous queens and America's First Lady Martha Washington along three costumes and headpieces or bonnets for each. Included are Martha, Queen Elizabeth I, Queen Margherita. Queen Marie Antoinette, Queen Isabella, Queen Victoria, Queen Louise, each drawn and water-colored by Elizabeth S. Tucker, printed by Frederick Stokes, along with an introductory booklet detailing the historical accuracy of the costumes and with directions on use and play. Excellent condition. American, circa 1895. $600/900

**133. American Cut Paper Dolls "Princes and Princesses" Drawn by E.S. Tucker**
7". The set includes 7 paper dolls and their costumes, each single-sided with easel back, comprising Louis with 3 costumes and 2 hats; Princes of Wales with 3 costumes and 1 hat; Friedrich with 3 costumes; Marguerite with 3 gowns; Wilhemina with 3 dresses; Princess with 3 dresses; and Mary with 3 gowns. All drawn and hand-colored by Elizabeth Stokes, published by Frederick Stokes. Very good to excellent condition. America. circa 1895. $400/600

**134. American "A Year of Paper Dolls" Drawn by E.S. Tucker**
7". A cardboard double-sided doll owns 12 double-sided costumes, 10 with an attached calendar for the year 1895, and each designed to represent a activity for that time of year. Included is a booklet detailing the background of the set, with instructions for cutting and assembly; it is recommended that at the beginning of each month another costume is but and the calendar month glued to it. Excellent condition, two costumes have missing stockings, two months missing calendars. Drawn and water-colored by Miss Elizabeth S. Tucker, published by Frederick Stokes, 1895. $300/400

Paper Dolls

### 135. French Uncut Paper Dolls from La Poupee Modele
10" x 6" sheets. Three cardboard sheets feature paper dolls representing Spring, Autumn and Winter, each with a double-sided paper doll, and two double-sided costumes. Labeled "Poupee Modele, 14 Rue Druout". French, from the popular children'a magazine, circa 1870. Excellent condition, uncut, some water spotting. $300/400

### 136. French Paper Dolls from La Poupee Modele
10" x 6" uncut sheet. Cardboard sheet featuring a double-sided paper doll along with two double-sided "flower costumes" and hats, labeled "La Poupee Modele, 52 Rue St. Georges Paris IX, Supplement au No. du 15 Juin 1909". Along with additional cut and assembled double-sided flower costumes from the same series, 10 dresses and 5 hats. Excellent condition. French, circa 1909. $200/250

### 137. French Uncut Paper Doll Sheet "Petit Costumier" by Pellerin
15" x 11". A large heavy paper sheet features one double-sided paper doll and costume, along with 4 double-sided bonnets and coiffures. Imagerie D'Epinal, Pellerin & Cie, No. 1058. French, circa 1876. Excellent condition except wear at bottom left corner. $200/250

**138. French Paper Doll Book "Belle Dames en Grand Toilette" Illustrated by JOB**
12.5" x 10". A hardbound book features 14 hand-drawn and water-colored plates featuring costumes through the ages right up to the present (circa 1900), with explanatory page alongside each. Each page is uncut and includes double-sided paper doll head and stick form, one double-sided costume, 2 hats, and an accessory. Illustrations by JOB, published by Hachette & Cie. Cover worn, paper doll pages excellent. France, circa 1900. $400/500

Paper Dolls

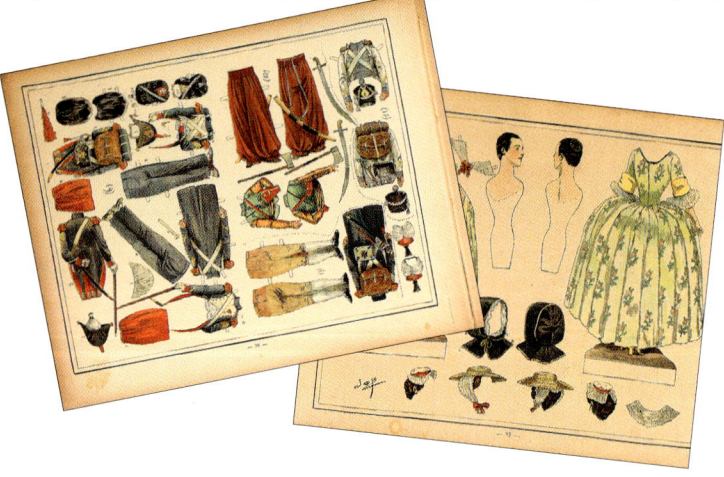

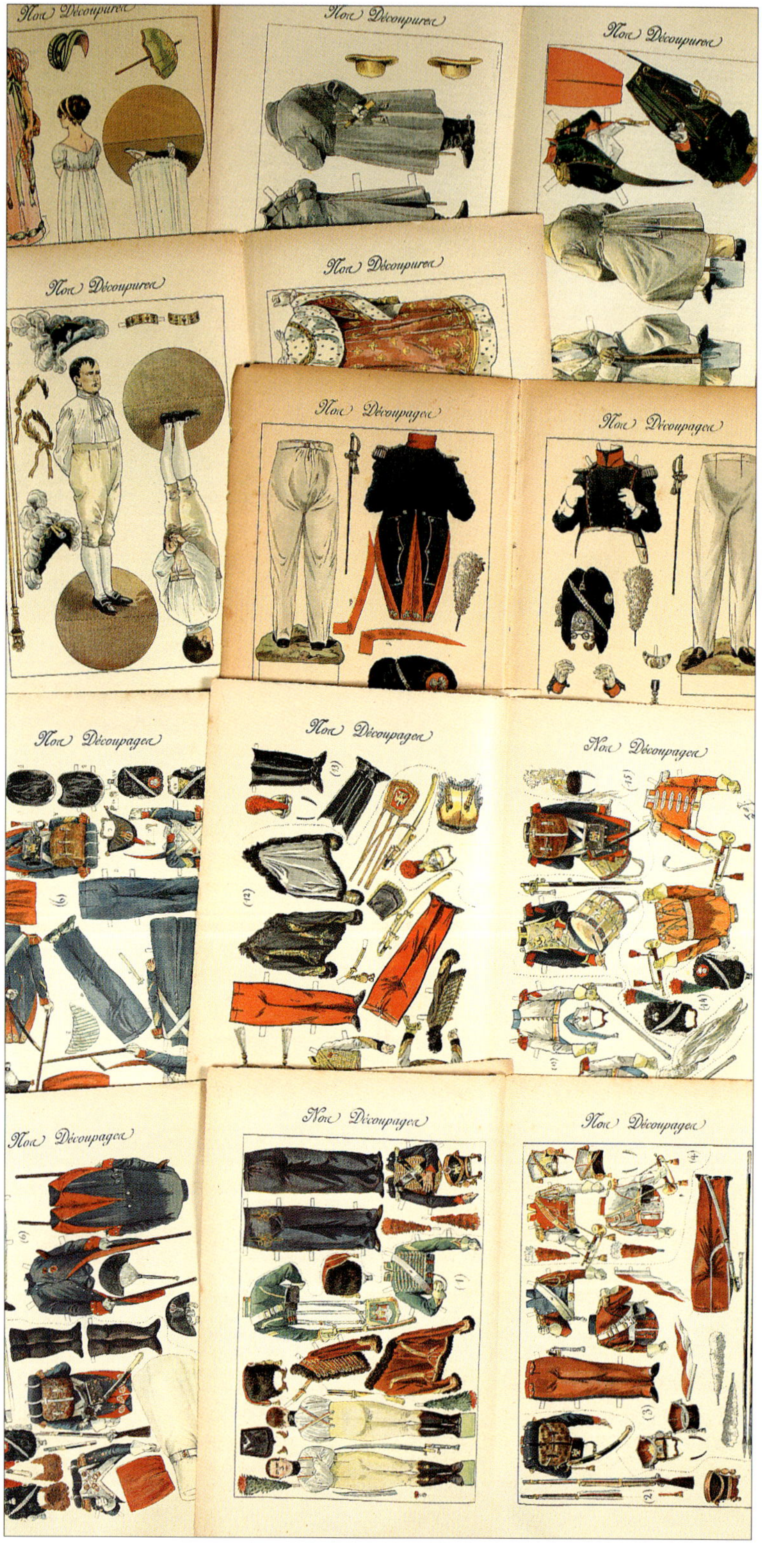

**139. French Paper Doll Book "L'Empereur, L'Imperatrice, La Garde"**
*Illustrated by JOB*
12.5" x 10". A hardbound book features 9 hand-drawn and water-colored paper doll pages featuring costumes of Napoleon, Josephine and member of the Garde Imperiale. 7 pages are uncut, the pages of Napoleon and Josephine have been cut but complete. Each features double-sided doll with costumes and numerous accessories. Illustrations by JOB, published by Hachette & Cie. Very good condition. France, circa 1900. $200/300

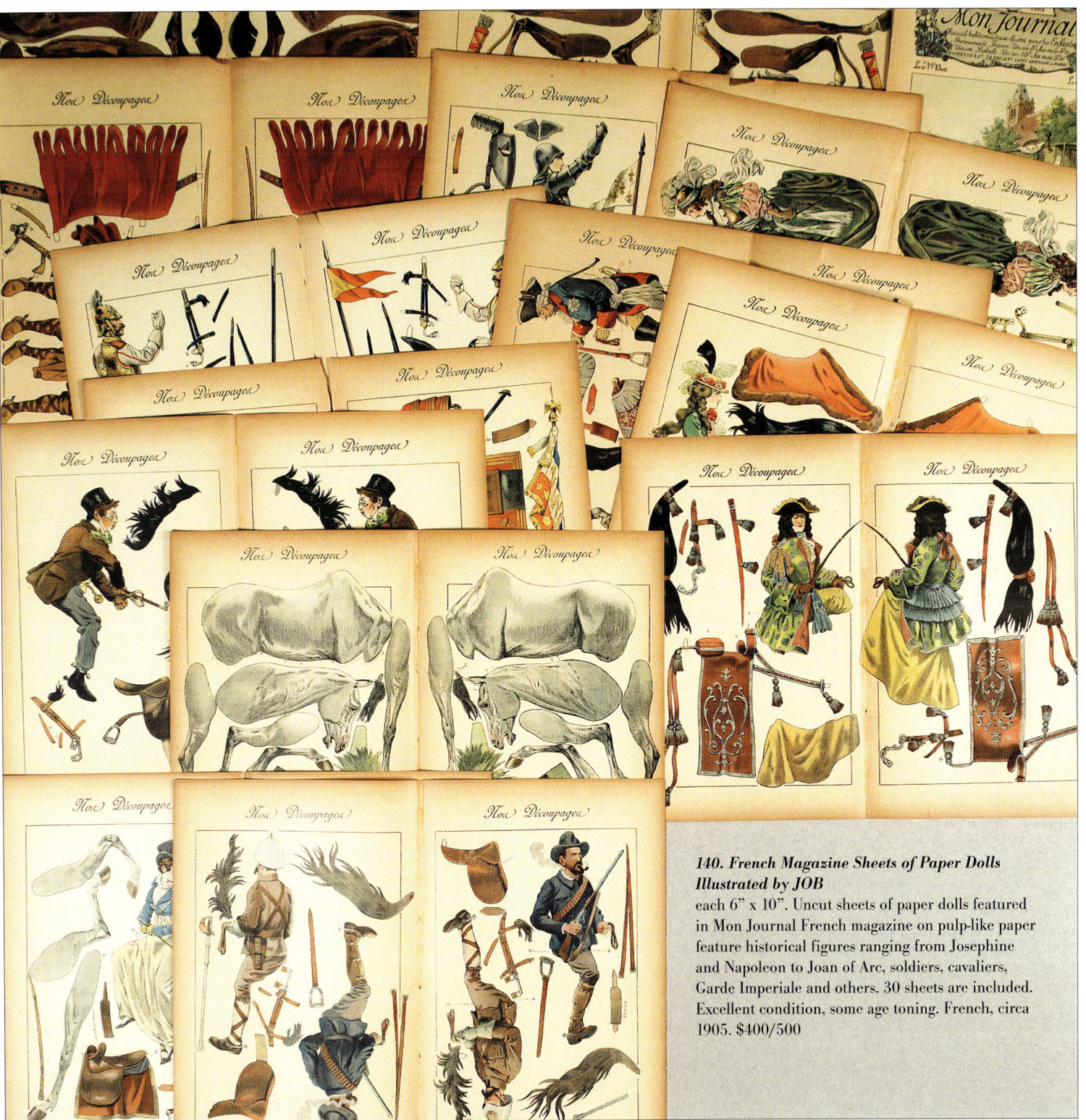

**140. French Magazine Sheets of Paper Dolls Illustrated by JOB**
each 6" x 10". Uncut sheets of paper dolls featured in Mon Journal French magazine on pulp-like paper feature historical figures ranging from Josephine and Napoleon to Joan of Arc, soldiers, cavaliers, Garde Imperiale and others. 30 sheets are included. Excellent condition, some age toning. French, circa 1905. $400/500

Paper Dolls

# Chapter IV. European Paper Dolls 1790-1860

**141. Various American Supplement Paper Dolls**
Including 8" x 11" uncut sheet of 1895 Bridal party from Boston Sunday Globe, four 8" x 10" uncut sheets of stick-body paper dolls from Boston Globe of 1895, and five cut paper dolls and costumes from Boston Sunday Globe. Good to excellent condition. $150/250

**142. American Paper Doll Costumes as Chicago Record Supplements**
Features 7" uncut sheets (7" x 11") from 1895, and 18 additional cut costumes from the same series. Excellent condition. 1895. $300/400

Paper Dolls

**143. American Paper Dolls as Boston Sunday Herald Supplements**
Includes one uncut and one cut 10.5" paper dolls, along with 17 uncut costumes, and 18 costumes, some with hats and accessories. The series covers 1895/1896. Excellent condition. $500/700

### 144. American Paper Dolls as Demorest Magazine Supplement
Includes one 8.5" paper doll, two sheets of uncut costumes, and five cut costumes. From Demorest Magazine, 1895. Very good condition. $200/250

### 145. Two American Supplement Paper Dolls
Including 8" x 10" uncut sheet of "Geraldine Farrar" from series "Paper Dolls of Famous Players" featuring costumes of her famous theatre roles, supplement of New York Sunday American, circa 1900; and double-sided cut paper doll and 2 costumes from Philadelphia Inquirer of June 1895. Excellent condition. $100/200

### 146. American Paper Doll "Little Louise" from Good Housekeeping
6.5" x 9.5" pages. Seven uncut pages featuring Little Louise, her siblings and her friends, in delicately rendered watercolors. Each page features a doll, costumes and accessories and playthings. Very good/excellent condition, spine edges rough. Circa 1909. $150/200

**147. American Paper Dolls as Sunday Supplements**
Featuring two 12" cut paper dolls, one uncut costume from The Sunday Sun with coupon for ordering dress pattern, dated 1905, two partially cut costumes, and 7 cut costumes. Good to excellent condition. 1905. $200/300

**148. American Paper Dolls "Polly's Paper Playmates"** *from The Boston Post* 8" x 10". Featuring 23 uncut pages each with at least one paper doll and superbly detailed costumes (from 2-5 costumes each) and accessories. Each page is based around a theme such as Cousin Janet at the Art Show or Sister Prue's Automobile Costume, and the costumes reflect the activity or theme. Each is labeled The Boston Post, 1910/1911. Very good to excellent condition. $700/1000

Paper Dolls

### 149. Rare 1897 Newspaper Supplement Paper Doll "My Ladye Faire Doll"
7". Several uncut pulp newspaper sheets depicts a fashionable lady in lingerie, along with wide circular skirt designed to be cut and "dressed" upon the doll in a dimensional manner. Also included are directions for assembly and one assembled and dressed doll. Marked "My Ladye Faire Doll" and New York Herald, 1897. Excellent condition. $200/300

### 150. 1902 Newspaper Supplement Paper Doll "Ready for the Promenade"
14" x 10" sheet. 9.5" doll. An uncut heavy card sheet portrays a paper doll woman in fashionable costume, along with an additional blouse, purse and hat, and with uncolored stole and directions for assembly. Labeled "Art Supplement, Ready for the Promenade" and N.Y. Journal, Sunday April 20th, 1902. Excellent condition. $100/200

### 151. 1903 Newspaper Supplement Paper Doll "Miss Dolly and Her Rainy Day Clothes"
14" x 10". 7" doll. An uncut sheet features two paper dolls of Miss Dolly in rainy day gear along with accessories and directions for making the dolls stand and for placing the umbrellas in their hands to be held securely. Marked "Cut out Supplement of the New York American and Journal, Sunday April 19th, 1903". Excellent condition, tiny corner tear. $100/200

**152. 1917 Newspaper Supplement Paper Dolls from the Chicago Tribune**
16" x 10" sheets. 7" dolls. Three uncut pulp paper sheets depict dolls from a series titled "Fold-A-Way" dolls, each with double-sided doll and 2 costumes and accessories along with directions for assembly. Included are The Bathing Girl, The Dancer and The Trained Nurse. Drawn by Penny Ross, and appearing in the Chicago Tribune from 1917/1919. Also included is one cut doll and costumes. Excellent condition. $200/250

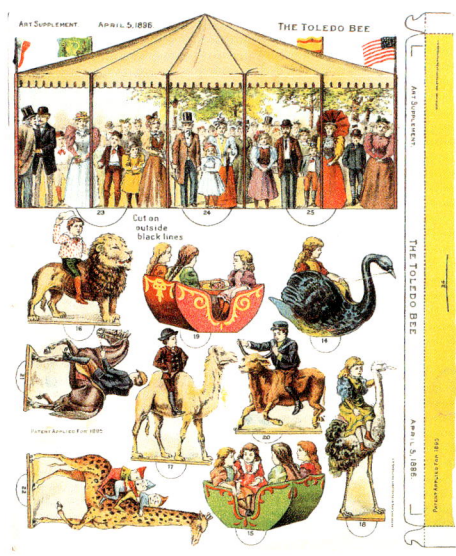

**154. 1896 Newspaper Supplement Paper Toy Carousel from The Toledo Bee**
17" x 10" sheet overall. An uncut cardboard sheet with center fold depicts on the left side a scene of people entering the fair grounds, and nine uncut vignettes of children on carousel animals or gondolas; the right page (not shown) is the base of the carousel and includes directions for assembly. Appearing in The Toledo Bee, April 5, 1896, one set of riders is a trio of Palmer Cox Brownies. Excellent condition except separated at center crease. $200/250

**153. 1919 Newspaper Supplement Paper Doll from The North American**
12.5" x 8.5". Two uncut card sheets depict "Fold-A-Way Color Toys" of animals and circus performers, designed to be cut and folded over, with color printed image on one side, and the other side designed to be colored by the user. Each piece includes a written description of the scene. Appearing in The North American of Philadelphia in 1919. Very good/excellent, some darkening and small wears on edges. $50/100

**155. 1915 Newspaper Supplements from The Syracuse Herald**
13" x 8". Six uncut sheets with dolls, 2 or more costumes and accessories for each and directions for assembly include a fashionable gentleman curiously named George Washington, Son Peter Age 5 along with auto, Daughter Martha Age 7, Little Bo-Peep along with sheep, Little Boy Blue, and Peter Pumpkin. Each signed copyright 1915 by S. Baxter. Appearing in The Herald, Syracuse, New York. Very good/excellent condition. $200/250

**156. 1912 Magazine Sheets by Carolyn Chester for The Delineator**
16" x 11". Six uncut magazine pages depict "Carolyn, Full-Base Paper Doll" and her little sister Betty, each page with a bountiful array of double-sided costumes and accessories. Designed by Carolyn Chester, the pages appeared in The Delineator in 1912. Very good/excellent condition. $200/250

**158. 1927 Magazine Sheets of Paper Dolls from US States**
11" x 14". Five uncut sheets each depict one paper doll with five costumes and other accessories, including Madeline of Maine, Carl of California, Texas Tom, Winifred of Wisconsin, and Katy of Kentucky. Drawn by Katherine Shane, the pages appeared in Woman's Home Companion in 1927. Very good/excellent condition. $100/150

**157. 1913 Magazine Sheets by Carolyn Chester for The Delineator**
16" x 11". Five uncut magazine pages depict "Round-Base Paper Dolls Given Historic Value by Mr. Corwin Knapp Linson" and includes the World Journey of the Butterick pattern, The First Butterick Pattern of 1863, and 3 others. Each page features double-sided paper dolls with wrap-around base and several costumes and accessories. Designed by Carolyn Chester, the pages appeared in The Delineator in 1913. Very good/excellent condition. $200/250.

**159. 1925 Magazine Sheets by Nandor Honti for McCall's**
9" x 14". Ten uncut sheets of double-sided dolls and costumes feature one or two dolls on each page along with a variety of costumes and accessories to define the particular theme being shown, ranging from Sister Nell Goes to a Party, to Two Jolly Playmates romp in the Park. Drawn by Nandor Honti for McCall's, 1926. Very good/excellent condition. $150/200

**160. 1923 Newspaper Supplements "The Angel Family" by Penny Ross**
15" x 12". Fourteen uncut pulp paper sheets depict members of The Angel Family ranging from adults to children, each sheet with 3 paper dolls and costumes, along with directions for play. One page offers 500 free 24" dolls to the 500 children who submit the best dressed paper dolls. Drawn by Penny Ross, the supplements appeared in The Chicago Tribune in 1922. Very good/excellent condition. $200/300

**161. Magazine Sheets of "Dolly Dingle" from Pictorial Review**
14" x 10". Fifteen uncut magazine pages depicting Dolly Dingle with costumes and accessories, along with related family members including Baby Brother, Little Cousin Leonard, Mother and Father during Wartime, and others. Drawn by Grace G. Drayton for Pictorial Review from 1917-1930. Along with a 12.5" x 10" paper doll book "Dolly Dingle at Play" with three loose pages of paper dolls, costumes and accessories (very worn, not shown). Good to very good condition. $300/400

**162. 1926 Magazine Sheets of "Peggy Pryde" from Pictorial Review**
14" x 10". Five uncut pages depicting flapper era child Peggy Pryde along with her Athletic Brother Phil, Cousin Carrie, Sister Patty and others, each sheet with one large doll and three costumes and accessories. The pages appeared in Pictorial Review in 1926. Excellent condition, few corner tears. $150/200

**163. 1920 Magazine Sheets of The Companion Paper Dolls**
16" x 11". Eight uncut sheets introduce a series of children from The Companion Series including Margery May, Tamaki, Marie Louise, Suzette and others each with 2 or 3 costumes and accessories and a storyline. Drawn by M. Emma Musselman, the pages appeared in 1920. Very good/excellent condition. $100/150

**164. 1922 Magazine Sheets of The Twins Series from Ladies Home Companion**
14" x 10" Eleven uncut sheets of Fold-A-Way dolls each featuring boy and girl twins with costumes and accessories to define their storyline, ranging from The Scotch Twins to The Eskimo Twins. Drawn by Jessie Louise Taylor, the pages appeared in the Ladies Home Companion in 1922. Very good condition. $100/200

**165. 1920's Magazine Sheets of Paper Dolls by Chiquet from Child Life**
12" x 9". Fifteen uncut sheets each featuring one doll and two costumes portray a fashionable child of the flapper era. The costumes were designed by Chiquet who also designed actual child's patterns that could be purchased from Child Life Pattern Department. Delicate pastel coloring, drawn by Driggs, the pages appeared in Child Life from 1925-1930. Excellent condition. $100/200

### 166. 1923/24 Magazine Sheets of *The Twins* by Frances Tipton Hunter
10" x 12". Four uncut sheets feature The Twins as newborns, and at ages 2, 4, and 7, each sheet with boy and girl dolls and various costumes and accessories to enhance the storyline. Drawn by Frances Tipton Hunter, the pages appeared in late 1923 and 1924. Excellent condition. $150/200

### 167. 1922/3 Magazine Sheets of "The Little Busybodies" by Frances Tipton Hunter
14" x 10.5". Six uncut sheets feature The Little Busybodies including Katy Curls, Squeezicks doll, Rogue Rob, Jolly Jane and others. Each sheet features one doll with five or more costumes and accessories and details of a "surprise" game. Drawn by Frances Tipton Hunter, the pages appeared in Woman's Home Companion. Excellent condition. $150/200

### 168. Miscellaneous Magazine Sheets of Paper Dolls
about 11" x 14". Including 1912 Mammy Cook drawn by Carolyn Chester, 1921 Dell from Delineator (2 sheets), 1933 Joan & Bill's Easter party by Lydia Fraser, 1919 Soldiers of 3 Wars and their Lasses from Delineator, 1918 Toinette La Petite drawn by Alida Clement, 1913 Baby Polly and her Irish Nurse drawn by Carolyn Chester, 1917 Mistress Mary drawn by Carolyn Chester; and 1915 Baby Bunting drawn by Catherine Hopkins. Very good/excellent. $150/200

# Chapter V. The New Century

**169. American Paper Dolls and Companion Books "The Little Colonel"**
Including three hardbound story books of The Little Colonel by Annie Fellows Johnston (viz. The Little Colonel, 1906 imprint; The Little Colonel's Chum, 1908 (1927 imprint); and The Little Colonel's Hero (1902, 1918 imprint). Along with The Little Colonel Doll Book featuring The Little Colonel with 9 costumes; Betty Lewis with 5 costumes, Kitty Walton with 5 costumes, Mary Ware with 9 costumes, Rob Moore with 2 costumes, Phil Tremont with 2 costumes, Malcolm McIntyre with 2 costumes, Keith McIntyre with 2 costumes, Miss Beck, and May Lilly with 2 costumes. First impression, published by Page 1910, paper dolls designed and painted by Mary G. Johnston, book autographed "Sincerely yours, Mary G. Johnston, Chautauqua 1911. Contents excellent, two loose pages, cover frayed. $600/900

**170. American Paper Doll Book "Mary Ware Doll Book"**
9.5" x 7". Hard bound book, designed as a companion to The Little Colonel Doll Book, written by Annie Fellows Johnston and designed and painted by W.M. Crocker, published by Page Company in 1914, this being a first impression. The 48 page book contains ten paper dolls and 38 costumes, each preserved uncut. Excellent condition. $600/900

**171. American Paper Dolls "Polly's Paper Playmates"**
10" x 8" sheets. A large folded panel of six 10" x 8" sheets depicting Polly with costumes for various national dances, The American Dance being featured on the cover. Each sheet includes at least 2 costumes with a wide variety of accessories. Also included are 11 individual sheets, some with newspaper supplement indicia such as Boston Post of 1911. Large panel excellent, individual sheets have varying wear. American, circa 1911. $400/500

**172. American Paper Doll Book, The Mary Frances Housekeeper" by Jane Eayre Fryer**
9" x 6.5". The hardbound book with paper jacket illustrated by Julia Greene contains 4 uncut pages of paper dolls and costumes and 14 pages of uncut furniture. The 253 page book has storyline, housekeeping tips, and other entertainments. Published by John Winston in 1914, first edition, the book has ink inscription by the author "The book for all girls (and boys) who love to 'play house'" along with her signature. Excellent condition, except jacket worn. $600/900

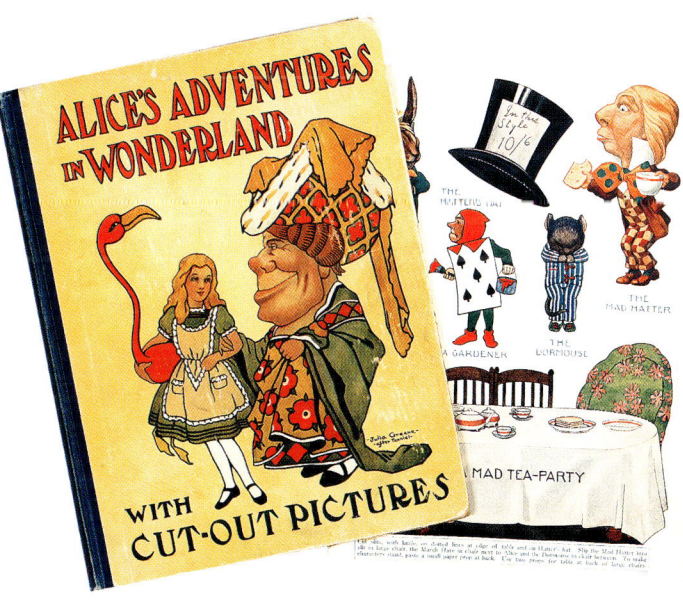

**173. American Paper Doll Book "Alice's Adventures in Wonderland"**
9.5" x 7.5" The hardbound book includes three uncut and one cut sheets of paper dolls and accessories to accompany the story line, painted by Julia Greene and Helen Pettes after Sir John Tenniel, published by Cupples & Leon in 1917, first edition. Excellent condition. $300/400

Paper Dolls

**174. American Paper Doll Book "The Dolls that You Love"**
19" x 12". The hardbound book features delicate watercolor drawings by L.R.S. Henderson and a storyline of five children and their nurse. Accompanying the book are cut paper dolls and costumes of the children and nurse. Copyright 1910 by L.W. Walter, published by Hamming Publishing of Chicago. Book worn, paper dolls excellent. $300/400

**175. American Paper Doll Book "Real Life in Dolly Land"**
16" x 10". Includes pages of illustrated and colored paper dolls and costumes along with line drawings of the same costumes designed for child play. Some costumes cut and missing. Stanton and Van Vliet, Chicago, copyright 1913 by C.C. Thompson. Good condition. $100/200

**176. Two American Paper Doll Books**
Including 12" x 10". Our Dollies Model Book with three pages of double-sided paper dolls and costumes, by McLoughlin Bros; and Dollies to Paint, Cut-out and Dress with five pages of colored paper dolls and costumes, and pages to color, by Saalfield. Fair/good condition. $100/200

**177. American Paper Doll "Miss Brown" by Stokes**
13" x 11". Two uncut cardboard sheets depict three paper dolls, Miss Brown with 3 costumes and hats, and The Nurse and The Governess each with 1 additional costume and hat. The sheets are from "The Treasure Trunk of Dollies", Frederick Stokes 1912. Excellent condition. $200/300

**178. German "Paper Dollies" for the English Market**
5". A partial box with lid depicting a child playing with paper dollies, contains boy and girl paper dolls with attached costumes, and one incomplete strip. Marked "Made in Germany" on reverse side. Excellent dolls and costumes, box broken. Circa 1915. $150/200

**179. English Paper Doll "Peggy and Her New Outfit" by Spears**
7". Features one single-sided easel back embossed paper doll with four costumes and one hat. Excellent condition. Spears, circa 1920. $100/150

Paper Dolls

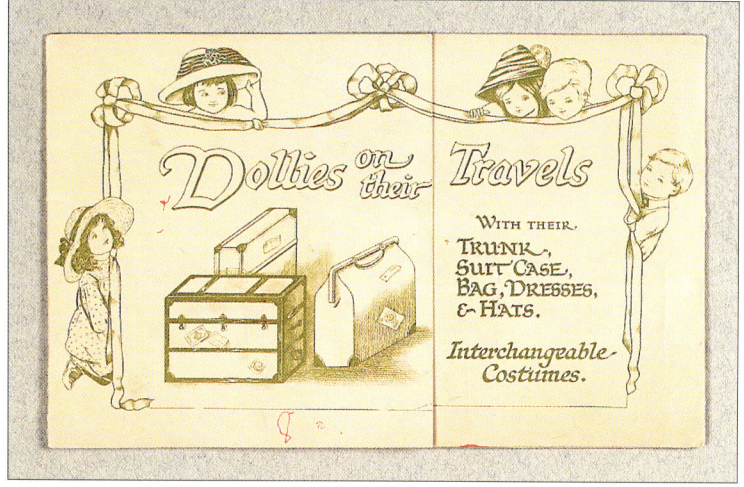

**180. English Paper Doll Set "Dollies on Their Travels" by Tuck**
9.5" x 6" booklet, 4" paper dolls. A folio booklet with well detailed cover design including suitcases and trunks, opens to reveal a background ocean scene and three paper dolls, each standing next to a valise or steamer trunk that contain extra paper doll costumes (4 costumes total). Excellent condition albeit incomplete. Marked Raphael Tuck. Circa 1920. $200/250

**181. English Paper Doll Set "Leslie Carter" by Raphael Tuck**
8". Heavy cardboard single-sided, easel back paper doll depicting the celebrity theatre actress of the late 19th century, along with four costumes from her most famous theatrical performances: three costumes from Zaza and one from The Heart of Maryland. Each labeled on the reverse, with Tuck signature and patent date of 1894. From Tuck's Famous Faces series. Circa 1895. $300/400

**182. American Sheet Paper Dolls by McLoughlin**
10.5" x 10.5". Comprising three uncut sheets, two of women, and one of baby, each with one single-sided paper doll and 5 costumes and accessories. Labeled Set A (C or D) McLoughlin Bros New York. Along with another woman from same series, cut with cut costumes. Excellent condition, edges darkened, one corner of baby sheet broken. Circa 1915. $200/250

**183. Two American Paper Dolls "Constance" and "Martha" from Woolworth Series**
20". Each is single-sided cardboard doll, each with three costumes and three hats. Very good condition, Constance missing easel and taped at center back. Circa 1918. $100/200

**184. Two American Paper Dolls "Jack" and "Modern Girl" from Woolworth Series**
20". Each is single-sided cardboard doll, each with three costumes and three hats. Very good condition. Circa 1918. $150/250

Paper Dolls

**185. Two American Paper Dolls "Peggy" and "Paul" from Woolworth Series**
20". Each is single-sided cardboard doll, Peggy with 3 costumes and 3 hats, Paul with 2 costumes and 1 hat. Good/very good condition. Circa 1918. $150/250

**186. Two American Paper Dolls "Betty" and "Priscilla" from Woolworth Series**
20". Each is single-sided cardboard doll, Priscilla with 3 costumes and 3 hats, Betty with 3 costumes and 1 hat. Very good condition. Circa 1918. $150/250

**187. Two American Paper Dolls "Ruth" and "Grace" from Woolworth Series**
20". Each is single-sided cardboard doll, Ruth with 3 costumes and 1 hat, Grace with 3 costumes and 3 hats. Very good condition. Circa 1918. $150/250

**188. Two American Paper Dolls "Jane" and "Colonial Doll" from Woolworth Series**
20". Each is single-sided cardboard doll, each with 3 costumes and 3 hats. Very good condition. Circa 1918. $150/250

**190. American Paper Doll Lady in Pink Dress in the Woolworth Style**
16". Single-sided cardboard doll depicting young woman, easel back with vignette base, along with two additional costumes enhanced with generous jewelry and purse accessories. Excellent condition. Circa 1917. $200/300

**191. American Paper Doll in the Woolworth Style**
16". Single-sided cardboard doll depicting a young girl with wind-blown hair, along with two additional costumes and two hats. Excellent condition. Circa 1918. $100/150

**192. Two American Paper Dolls "Helen" and "Lillian" from Woolworth Series**
20". Each is single-sided cardboard doll, Helen with 3 costumes and 3 hats along with original (frail) envelope, Lillian with 3 costumes and 3 hats. Excellent condition. Circa 1918. $200/300

**193. Two American Paper Dolls "Dorothy" and "Ethel" from Woolworth Series**
20". Each is single-sided cardboard doll, Ethel with 3 costumes and 2 hats, Dorothy with 3 costumes and 3 hats. Very good/excellent condition, Dorothy has neck repair. Circa 1918. $150/300

**194. Five American Paper Dolls from Woolworth Series**
20". Each is single-sided cardboard doll, including Beatrice with 3 costumes and 3 hats, Jessie with 3 costumes and 3 hats (neck repair), Lucy with 3 costumes and 3 hats (1 costume and 1 hat torn), Florence with 3 costumes and 3 hats (neck bent), and Geraldine with 3 costumes and 1 hat (neck repair). Very good/excellent except as noted. Circa 1918. $400/600

**194A. Five American Paper Dolls from Woolworth Series**
20". Each is single-sided cardboard doll, including Vincent with 2 costumes and 2 hats (face and hand repair), Marion with 3 costumes and 3 hats (neck bend), Romeo with 1 costume (repaired hand), Mabel with 3 costumes and 2 hats (neck bend), and Alice with 3 costumes and 2 hats (neck repair). Very good condition except as noted. Circa 1918. $300/500

# Chapter VI. Postcard & Greeting Card Paper Dolls

**195. American Postcard Paper Doll Book "The Paper Doll Family"** 6" x 3.5". A heavy cardboard book with colorful cover contains 10 interior postcard pages depicting the five family members (Mother, Father, Baby, Sister, Brother) each with 2 pages of doll, costumes and accessories, along with additional costumes and toys for Baby on the back cover. Excellent condition. Circa 1915. $200/300

**196. Various Postcard Paper Dolls** 5" x 3". Ten uncut paper doll postcards include Marie Louise for Buchanan Post Card Co (postmark 1922 on reverse), Fletcher Cut Out Post Card, Girl from Toy Town Series by W.E. Mack, English Bobby from Toy Town Series by W.E. Mack, Peter Pan from Town Town Series by W.E. Mack, two advertising cards featuring Raphael Tuck miniature paper dolls (one postmarked 1911), two matching postcards of Cinderella and Aladdin, and one punch-out card of little boy on hobby horse. Fair/excellent. Early 20th century. $200/300

**197. Eleven English Postcard Paper Dolls and Furniture by Raphael Tuck**
5" x 3". Including six postcards from The Dolls' House Furniture "Oilette" Series along with original envelope for one, three postcards of children (Little Pamela, Jack A Dandy, and Jack at Play, one postmarked 1921), and two punch-out cards from Fairy Land Panorama Series. Very good to excellent condition. Raphael Tuck, circa 1920. $300/500

**198. Five Easter Egg Greeting Cards with Paper Doll and Costumes**
5"l, card, 4.5" paper doll. Five egg-shaped greeting cards with delicate Springtime drawing and poem telling about "surprise" inside the card, each contain inside a paper doll (two bunnies, one chick, and two girls) along with a miniature envelope containing costumes. Excellent condition. Circa 1920's. $200/300

Paper Dolls

**199. Sixteen Greeting Card Paper Dolls**
Including Get Well, Birthday, and various holiday cards, each containing a paper doll and costumes, all in fine uncut condition. Circa 1930's. $200/400

**200. Thirty-Five Greeting Card Paper Dolls**
Including Get Well, Birthday, Valentine's Day and numerous other special occasion, each card containing a paper doll or paper animal presented in various imaginative designs, along with costumes and accessories. Excellent uncut condition. Circa 1930/1940. $400/500

*Lot 200 detail.*

Paper Dolls

# Chapter VII. Advertising Paper Dolls

**201. American Advertising Paper Dolls from Enameline**
5". The die-cut tent-style collection includes the complete set of 9 College Colors paper dolls, complete Flower Set, and five various including monkey, cat, girl with doll and American flag, and two flower children. Excellent condition, one has neck bend. Published by J.L. Prescott Co, New York. Early 20th century. $300/500

**202. American Advertising Paper Doll for Borazine**
3" x 4.5" cards. The set includes two uncut paper dolls and five uncut costumes, created for the Larkin Company. Early 20th century. $100/150

**203. American Advertising Paper Doll "Alice Thrifty" from Larkin**
5". The set includes one uncut paper doll, Alice Thrifty, and four uncut costumes indicating that the same costume for a real person can be purchased from the Larkin catalog. Also included is original envelope and coupon for Larkin playhouse. Excellent condition. Circa 1920. $300/400

**205. American Advertising Paper Doll Family from Blackwell Tobacco**
5" mother. The cut and partially cut set includes approximately 60 pieces including costumes, accessories, playthings and more. Excellent condition. Late 19th/early 20th century. $400/500

Paper Dolls

**206. American Advertising Paper Dolls, "Nursery Rhymes", for Lion's Coffee**
5". Thirty-eight die-cut paper dolls depict characters from favorite nursery rhymes or fairy tales, and advertise for Lion's Coffee. Late 19th/early 20th century. Very good/excellent condition. $500/700

**207. American Advertising Paper Dolls, "Doll House Series", for Lion's Coffee**
A large assortment of paper dolls, costumes, vignettes, room settings, comprising a mostly complete set of the Lion Coffee Doll House collection. Very good/excellent condition. Late 19th/early 20th century. $350/500

Paper Dolls

**208. American Advertising Paper Dolls, "Occupational Series" for Lion's Coffee**
Fifteen sets of occupational postcards present a vivid portrait of turn-of-the-20th century professions including cobbler, cabinet marker and photographer, each with primary paper doll figure and various die-cut "customer" paper dolls and accessories. Good/Excellent condition, mostly complete. Late 19th/early 20th century. $300/400

**209. Rare Set of American Advertising "People Animals" for McLaughlin Coffee** An amusing set of die-cut domestic animal "dolls" with wonderful die-cut people costumes for each. The collection is complete, excepting the hats. Excellent condition. Late 19th/early 20th century. $500/800

Paper Dolls

**210. American Advertising Paper Dolls "Activity Series" for McLaughlin Coffee**
Fifteen sets of paper dolls portraying various activities from doing laundry to taking a carriage ride, each include paper dolls, costumes, and various accessories or vignettes to complete the scene. Mostly complete. Excellent condition. Late 19th/early 20th century. $400/500

**211. American Advertising Paper Dolls, "Cape Series" for *McLaughlin Coffee***
5.5". Nine different paper dolls with "wing" capes designed to wrap-around during play, include both boys and girls, double-children, babies and others. Good/excellent, 1 wing missing. Late 19th/early 20th century. $200/300

**212. American Advertising Paper Dolls and Costumes for *McLaughlin Coffee***
Including 13 paper dolls of ladies, gentlemen, young girls, all with at least one costume. Very good/excellent condition. Late 19th/early 20th century. $200/300

**213. Very Large Sampling of American Advertising Paper Dolls by McLaughlin**
Including at least 50 different paper dolls from various series, each with at least one or two costumes. Very good to excellent condition. Late 19th/early 20th century. $400/500

**214. American Advertising Paper Dollhouse for Maple Sisters Cereal**

Includes two 13" x 16" uncut sheets of Living Room and Bedroom, three cut sheets of nursery, bathroom, and dining room, six 13" x 11" uncut sheets of dolls, wall pieces, costumes and furniture for various rooms, one 13" x 7" sheet of two dolls and costumes, and other cut dolls and costumes. The reverse of each sheet includes information on the entire series, and advertising for Mapl-Flake Cereal. One sheet was given free with two packages of cereal. Good to excellent condition, some water staining on bathroom sheet. Early 20th century. $700/900

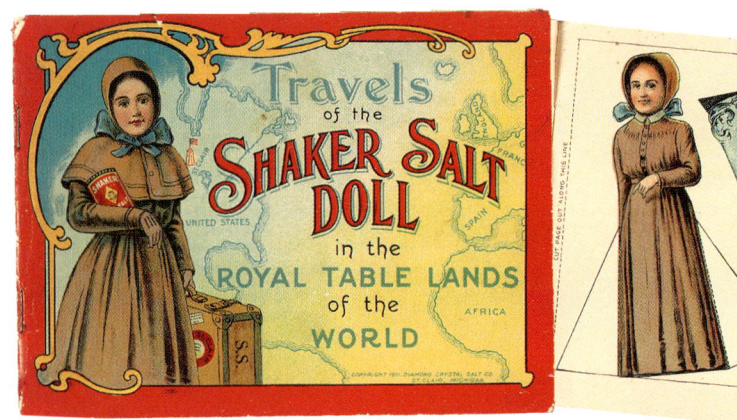
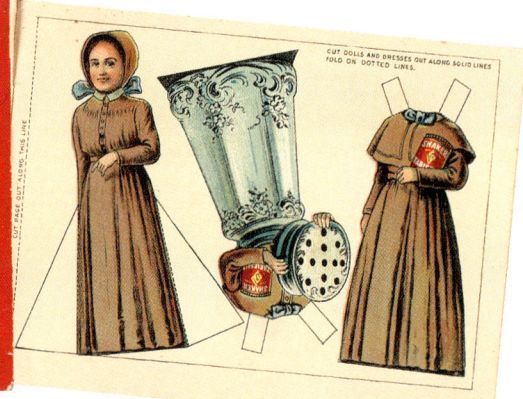

**215. American Advertising Paper Doll Booklet for Shaker Salt**
7" x 5". A colorful booklet tells the tale of The Little Shaker lady as she travels the world, and includes 8 uncut pages of paper dolls and costumes based upon these travels, and including The Little Shaker Lady herself. Copyright 1911 for Diamond Crystal Salt. Excellent condition. $300/400

**216. American Advertising Paper Dolls for Jayne's Hair Products**
Including 3.4" x 6" booklet with six pages of uncut dolls and costumes, along with advice on hair care. And 13" x 6" uncut four-panel fold-out sheet with two stick-body dolls and their uncut costumes. Excellent condition, booklet unbound. Circa 1915. $200/300

**217. American Advertising Paper Dolls "The Greatest Show on Earth" for Holsum and Sanatara Bread**
5.5" x 4". A colorful folio with circus theme contains six 4" x 5" cards of circus performer or animal paper dolls and accessories. Copyright 1919 by M&S Co. Very good condition. $150/250

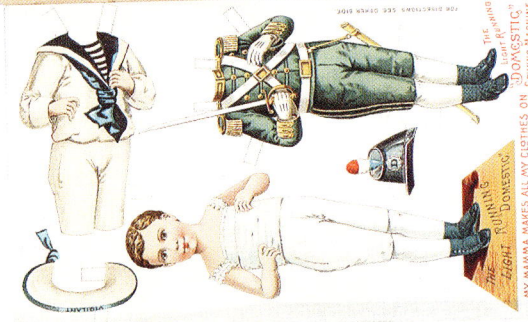

**218. American Advertising Paper Dolls for Pillsbury Flour**
Including two 8" x 6" uncut sheets with stick-body paper dolls (one Russian, one Japanese) in vignette setting featuring Pillsbury flour sacks, each with two costumes. A long with The Forbes Doll with three costumes and Pillsbury Flour apron: three additional uncut sheets of dolls and costumes, and a number of cut dolls and costumes. Good to excellent. Circa 1910. $150/250

**219. Two American Advertising Paper Doll Cards for Sewing Machines**
each about 3" x 5". Includes uncut boy paper doll with two costumes for The Light Running Domestic sewing machine, and uncut girl with two costumes, bonnets and accessories for Singer. Excellent condition. Circa 1895. $150/200

**220. American Advertising Paper Dolls for Worcester Salts**
6". Includes 6 nursery rhyme single-sided dolls with fold-back bases, two tent-style double-sided dolls with 1 dress, and easel-back child holding a doll. All with advertising for Worcester Salts on the reverse. Very good to excellent condition. Circa 1890. $150/200

Paper Dolls

**221. Large Collection of Advertising Paper Dolls for O.N.T. Clark Thread**
Including complete "Minuet Series" of ten paper dolls and one piano; 9 paper dolls from the Soldier Doll Series; and three double-sided heads, and six single head, along with 11 costumes each with accessory such as doll in carriage, birdcage, rake, or such. Each with advertising for O.N.T. Thread. Good to excellent condition. Circa 1900. $300/400

**222. American Advertising Paper Doll for Gordon Socks**
7". Mechanical die-cut paper doll that opens and closes eyes when paper stick at base is moved up and down. Advertising for "See my Gordon Socks" on front. Excellent condition. $100/150

### 223. American Advertising Paper Dolls for Sewing Machines

Including 8" single-sided easel back lady with advertising for Singer Sewing Machines along with two dresses, wedding gown and veil; and 5" x 8.5" beautiful paper doll trade card, uncut, for New Home Sewing Machine, featuring a double-sided paper doll with separate body having defined space for placement of head and hands, along with two double-sided heads (younger and older woman). Card very fine, Singer lady has neck bend, costumes excellent. Circa 1895. $300/400

### 224. American Advertising "Fairy Tale" Paper Dolls for Stollwerck's Cocoa

5". The set includes 8 girl paper dolls, 6 boy paper dolls, and one Puss in Boots, each with separate shoulder head and slip-over costume with advertising for Stollwerck's Cocoa on the reverse side. Further advertising on the interior describes the set of "Little Statuette" dolls, and the name of each fairy tale figure is shown on the front. Very good to excellent condition. Circa 1895. $300/400

### 225. American Advertising Emperors and Empresses Paper Dolls

5.5". 8 paper dolls feature royal figures from round the world, with double-sided slip-over costumes. No advertising. Good condition, back of four heads missing. Circa 1900. $50/100

**226. American Advertising Paper Dolls for None-Such Mincemeat**
5.5". The set includes five dolls with stick bodies, three-piece costumes (blouse, skirt and hat) for five dolls including Spanish, Swiss, Japanese, French, and American; and two-piece costumes (blouse and skirt) for 3 dolls (Russian, Turkish, and German). Each of the stick figures include advertising for None-Such Mincemeat. Very good condition. Circa 1895. $300/400

**227. Four Advertising Paper Doll Cards**
Including two 3" x 5" cards of boy and girl, each with two costumes and hats, for Western & Southern Life Insurance Co; punch-out postcard doll depicting little girl with mandolin for Henry Goldsmith Musical Instruments and Sheet Music; and 7" x 7" paper furniture sheet for Bush and Gerts Piano Co. Excellent condition, one corner tear on furniture sheet. Circa 1910. $150/250

**228. American Advertising Paper Dolls for Barbour Irish Thread**
5". Ten paper dolls each featuring a separate head and double-sided slip-over costume with advertising for Barbour Irish Thread. Excellent condition. Circa 1895. $100/150

**229. American Advertising Cards for Estey Organ**
6". Includes six paper dolls including an amusing set of four side-glancing roguish boys with advertising for Estey Organ. Very good to excellent condition. Circa 1910. $100/150

**231. American Advertising Fold-Over Sheets from Willimantic Threads**
6" x 5.5". Four single fold sheets feature two girls and two boys, each with several costumes and a myriad of accessories and toys. Very good condition, some darkening, one is partially cut. Circa 1900. $150/200

**230. American Advertising "Elsie Dinsmore" Paper Dolls**
17" x 8" folio opened. 6.5" doll. Including a six panel folding brochure (not shown) that features Elsie Dinsmore along with ten dresses and advertises that "You can get a real dress just like this one at our store". Along with a similar 6.5" named "Kathryn" with 8 costumes; 7" older child with 9 costumes (in one she holds a doll, in another she holds a Kewpie); 8" girl labeled Elsie Dinsmore with 13 costumes; and a 7.5" girl (badly bent) with 8 costumes. Excellent except as noted. Circa 1920. $500/700

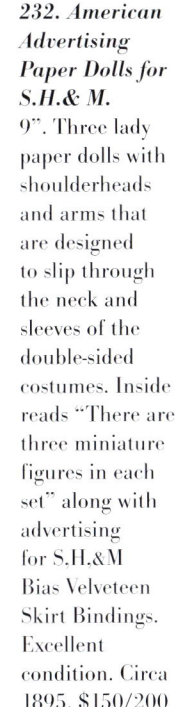

**232. American Advertising Paper Dolls for S.H.& M.**
9". Three lady paper dolls with shoulderheads and arms that are designed to slip through the neck and sleeves of the double-sided costumes. Inside reads "There are three miniature figures in each set" along with advertising for S.H.&M Bias Velveteen Skirt Bindings. Excellent condition. Circa 1895. $150/200

**234. American Advertising Paper Dolls for Diamond Dye**
5". Five single-sided easel back paper dolls depict a young girl in various activities, viz. playing with doll, with bird cage, and such. Each with advertising for Diamond Dyes. Excellent condition. $100/150

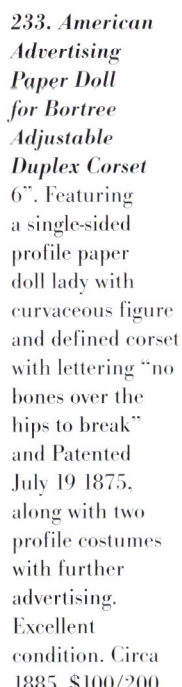

**233. American Advertising Paper Doll for Bortree Adjustable Duplex Corset**
6". Featuring a single-sided profile paper doll lady with curvaceous figure and defined corset with lettering "no bones over the hips to break" and Patented July 19 1875, along with two profile costumes with further advertising. Excellent condition. Circa 1885. $100/200

**235. American Advertising Paper Dolls, The Wedding Party, for O.N.T. Threads**
5". The set includes four thick cardboard uncut cards of Groom, Bride, Preacher, and Bridesmaid, along with cut fold-over paper doll of bride (?) from later set, also O.N.T. Very good to excellent. Circa 1920. $100/150

Paper Dolls

**236. Group of Various Advertising Paper Dolls**
Includes 6" lady advertising Sangria, 5" profile wrap-around lady advertising Chicoree A La Bergere, 3.5" wrap-around girl advertising Baker's Cocoa; 4.5" double-sided Koveralls Boy with different and extra costume on each side; group of animals with people costumes (no advertising), 7.5" cut-out dog and cat for Lion's Coffee, 8" cut-out dog for Lion's Coffee; Squirrel uncat paper doll for Spalding Bread, and 3" x 5" card of French Boy from Auerbach's Sweet Milk Chocolate. Very good to excellent. Early 20th century. $300/400

# Chapter VIII. Post WWI

**237. American Box Set of "My Sweet Dollies" by Gabriel**
4" x 8" box. Contains four uncut 7" paper dolls on heavy cardboard sheets, seven sheets of uncut costumes on white paper, four sheets of uncut costumes on pulp paper, and other cut costumes. The box contents list 2 dolls, so others are added. Marked Saalfield Publ Co. Akron, Ohio, with illustration of the doll. Box a bit worn, contents excellent. Circa 1920. $100/150

**238. Boxed Sets of Paper Dolls**
Including 4" x 5" box titled "Play with Me" with cut dolls and costumes, marked No.350K; 6" x 9" box "Fairy Tales" with three dolls and a myriad of costumes, marked Series No. 387; and a miniature envelope titled "My Pretty Dolly", Series No. 150, with 3.5" doll, 3 costumes and 3 hats. Two boxed sets are incomplete, boxes worn, contents very good. Envelope set is complete and excellent. Circa 1910. $100/150

**239. American Box Set of "My Dolly Cousin Kate" by Gabriel**
11" x 5" box. 9" doll. Includes cardboard doll marked D-90 Cousin Kate, along with four costumes and matching hats, with original labeled box. And 6.5" Cousin Marguerite with 3 costumes and two hats in original envelope labeled "Comfort", Augusta, Me., with illustration of the doll. Box very worn, doll and costumes excellent. Circa 1920's. $100/150

Paper Dolls 145

**241. German Paper Dolls and Costumes**
5.5"- 9". Featuring six paper dolls of various sizes, along with a large collection of cut costumes. Germany, circa 1920. Very good/excellent condition. $100/150

**240. American Paper Doll Book "Curly-Locks"**
21" x 9" book. 19" dolls. Includes two heavy cardboard punch-out dolls with attached easel stands (on front and back covers), along with pages of punch-out cardboard costumes. All uncut, some cover wear at edges, dolls and costumes excellent. Marked "Copyright Charles E. Graham & Co, Newark, N.J., New York. 0229". Circa 1920. $150/200

**242. American Paper Dolls by Gabriel**
Including 9" Susan with mechanical blinking eyes that operate by moving hair bow, along with one uncut costume labeled "Susan's Party Dress", an easel-back girl with bobbed hair, four costumes including a dress holding a doll, 3 hats; and (not shown) partial book and cover "Dainty Dollies". Two paper dolls and costumes excellent, book very poor condition. Gabriel, circa 1920. $100/200

### 243. American Embroidery Paper Dolls from Kaufmann & Strauss
9" dolls. Included in their original envelopes with instructions for use are four paper dolls from the Old Homestead Series, viz. Sisters Ruth, Helen, Mary and Brother Jack, each with four costumes and four hats. Each costume has perforated embroidery pattern on the reverse side indicating how the child might learn to embroider, and the envelopes indicate that the sets could be acquired by sending in coupons from Old Homestead Coffee. Marked "Copyright 1915 by Kauffmann & Strauss, N.Y., Patent No 1067923." Pulp paper envelopes very worn, dolls and costumes near mint. $300/500

### 244. American Paper Dolls "Dorothy Dimple and her Friends" by George Jacobs
9" x 14" folio envelope. A large folio with sepia tinted illustration of Gibson Girl style child playing with paper dolls is labeled "Dorothy Dimple and Her Friends, Paper Dolls of Many Nations by Cushman Parker, Contents Copyrighted by The Bodley Press Associates, Springfield, Mass, Published by George W. Jacobs, Philadelphia" and contains five envelopes each stamped Wilber Jacobs. Each envelope has hand-lettered name of cut doll and costumes inside: Dorothy's Japanese friend, Dorothy's sister Sarah, Dorothy Dimple's Next Door Neighbor Alice, and Dorothy Dimple, and each owns a nice selection of costumes. Cover spotted, contents excellent albeit cut. Circa 1915. $200/300

### 245. American Paper Doll Book and Sheets
Including Mother Goose Cut-Out Picture Book with two 9" paper dolls, Little Bo Peep and Little Red Riding Hood, along with one page of costumes for each. And three uncut sheets of Toy-kins, Heroes of Storybook Land, including Mother Rabbit, Peter Rabbit, and Sister Rabbit, patented 1917/18 by Esther Swetland, printed by Christ-Color Printing Engraving, Inc of Rochester New York. Fair/good condition. Circa 1917. $100/150

Paper Dolls

**246. *American Paper Dolls Drawn by Margaret Hays***
Including 10" x 13" book "Fairy Favorite" (No 671 copyright 1913 by M.A. Donohue) with three pages of paper dolls and costumes; 10" x 13." "The Nursery Favorite" (No 672, Copyright 1915 by M.A, Donohue) with six pages of flower-named paper dolls and costumes, both with beautiful cover designs. Along with 5 uncut sheets of flower-named paper dolls identical to those in the book. All art work by noted illustration Margaret Hays. Circa 1915. Fairy Favorite worn and incomplete, other book and sheets excellent. $150/250

**247. *American Paper Doll Book "Fairies from Fay-Land"***
8´ x 12" book. Containing a number of uncut, uncolored pages designed to cut and paint, featuring fantasy figures. Designed and Illustrated by Florence Pettee, published by Albert Whitman, 1922. Very good condition. $50/100

**248. *American Cut Paper Dolls and Costumes "Flapper Fanny"***
Comprising 13.5" Flapper Fanny adult lady with 9 cut costumes, 9.5" younger sister with wide-eyed expression and 10 cut costumes, 9.5" brother with costume elements, and several costumes for smaller paper doll, along with cut-out automobile front and a gas pump. Excellent condition. Whitman, circa 1920's. $50/100

**249. American Paper Doll "Tommy Tom" by Hubbell-Leavens**
17". A heavy cardboard easel-back paper doll in Scout costume along with clown and sailor costume, and a hat for each costume, along with original glassene envelope labeled "Tommy Tom, No. 4". Excellent condition, vibrant color. Hubbell-Leavens, circa 1920's. $100/150

**250. American Paper Dolls "Billy Boy" and "Dolly Dimple" by Hubbell-Leavens**
17". A heavy cardboard easel-back paper boy doll has four costumes and one hat, and girl has four costumes and five hats. Fair condition, some soil and bends. Hubbell-Leavens series of 1920's. $100/150

**251. Two American Paper Dolls by Hubbell-Leavens**
each 12". Depicting young toddler, and brunette haired young girl with red hair bows, each with wide easel back, and including a wide selection of costumes and hats. Excellent condition, beautiful coloring. Hubbell-Leavens series of 1920's. $100/200

**252. Two American Paper Dolls by Hubbell-Leavens**
each 12". Depicting 2 young children, boy and girl, each with wide easel back, and including a wide selection of costumes and hats. Excellent condition, lovely coloring is well preserved. Hubbell-Leavens, series of 1920's. $100/200

***253. American Paper Doll "Dolly Dolly" by Hubbell-Leavens***
12". Featuring a single-side easel-back cardboard doll with three costumes including unusual winged disguise and Scottish costume, along with original envelope showing doll in Scottish costume, and a book cover for Dolly Dimple. Envelope worn, doll and costumes excellent. Hubbell-Leavens 1920's series. $100/200

***254. American Boxed Set of "The Dimple Doll Family" by Gabriel***
7". Included in original box with illustration on the cover are three cut paper dolls and 14 uncut sheets of individual paper dolls. Samuel Gabriel, No. D-126. Costumes excellent, some bending on dolls, box sturdy but faded. Circa 1920's. $100/200

***255. English Paper Doll "Alice" by Raphael Tuck***
13". Cardboard paper doll with easel back and neck slit, along with three additional costumes and bodies. Marked Raphael Tuck, patented 1894. Excellent condition. Circa 1900. $150/200

***256. English Paper Doll "Sonny Jim"***
9.5". Cardboard paper doll of young lad holding a rabbit, along with 6 costumes and 5 hats, including Native American costume. In original glassene envelope marked No. 31 C/W. Excellent condition except easel missing and neck bend. $100/150

**257. American Boxed Set Paper Doll "Chubby Cubby" by American Colortype**
9.5". Cardboard paper doll of brown teddy bear with amber eyes, easel-back, along with three costumes including Native American with feathered headdress, pirate, and sailor, 2 hats, and seven accessories. With original box with bright lithographed cover marked "Chubby Cubby". American Colortype Company, Chicago, Illinois. Bear and costumes excellent, box cover has great colors and image, however box is broken. Circa 1920. $250/350

**258. American Paper Dolls "Pretty Kitty" and "Dandy Doggie" by American Colortype**
11" dolls. Including uncut sheet of Kitty along with two uncut sheets of fancy dress-up people costumes, along with cut Doggie paper doll along with three hats, two accessories, one being a wonderful Scottish golfer costume. Each with original envelope printed in vibrant colors with amusing detail. American Colortype Company, Chicago, Illinoise. Excellent condition, few edge tears on Doggie envelope. Circa 1920. $450/600

**259. German Boxed Set Paper Dolls "Playmates"**
5". Contained within their original box labeled "Playmates, 4 Dainty Dolls with 3 sets of interchangeable costumes" are 4 easily back paper dolls, along with 10 costumes each featuring a variation of arm pose and accessories, 2 separate hats, and an unusual folio with opening "window" labeled "Dolly at the window". Box is marked Series No. 372, and follo is marked S&C. Dolls and costumes excellent, box worn. Germany, circa 1920's. $100/200

**260. German Uncut Sheets of Paper Dolls**
9" x 7" sheets. Four uncut sheets each with different paper doll and 3 to 5 costumes and matching headdresses. The costumes reflect traditional or folklore style costumes and are accented with small floral bouquets of that region. Excellent condition with vibrant colors. Germany, 1920's. $150/250

**261. Two German Boxed Sets of Mechanical Eye Paper Dolls**
Including "Dolly Dear" in 5" x 9" box with image of doll on front cover, 7" doll whose eyes open and close by moving easel back up and down, with 3 costumes including one holding a doll, 3 hats and teddy bear and rose bouquet, box marked Socolu, No 392A; and 5" x 12" box with image of girl holding a sleeping eye baby, containing 11" doll whose eyes open and close by moving easel up and down, along with one nighgown holding teddy bear, and one night cap, marked S&C, Series No 386. Dolly Dear excellent, Dolly Mine doll and costume excellent albeit box worn and set incomplete. Germany, circa 1920's. $500/700

Paper Dolls

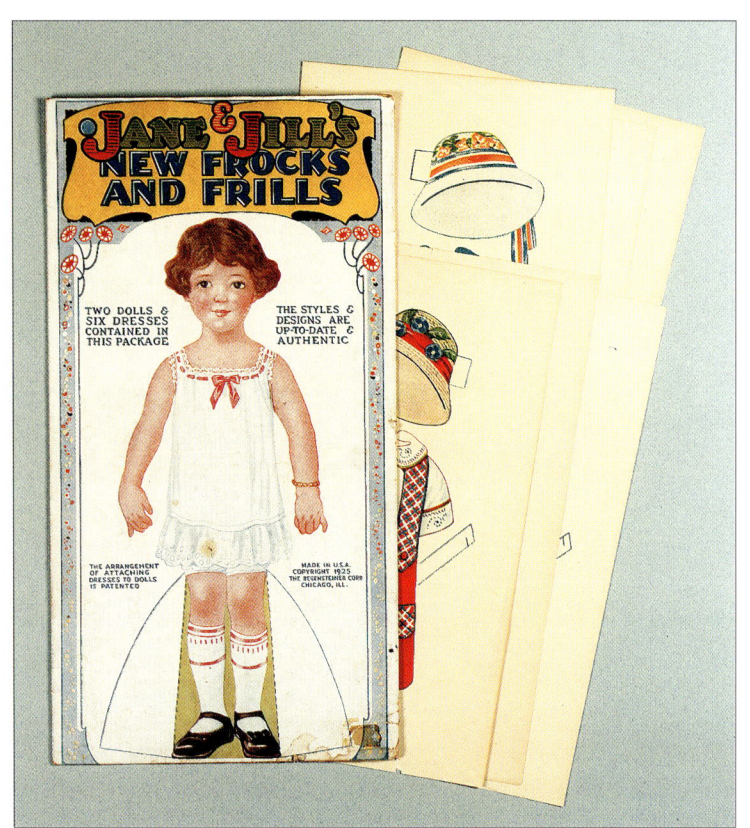

**262. American Paper Dolls "Jane & Jill" by Regensteiner**
13" dolls. A heavy cardboard envelope, 15" x 8", with vibrantly printed cover features uncut paper dolls on front and back, along with six uncut sheets of costumes. The envelope is marked "Jane & Jill's New Frocks and Frills", "Made in USA Copyright 1925 The Regensteiner Corp, Chicago Ill.". Excellent condition. 1925. $150/200

**264. Two American Paper Dolls by American Colortype**
12". Including girl with three costumes and three hats, and boy with three costumes. Possibly "Corinne" and "Howard". Excellent condition. Circa 1920's. $75/125

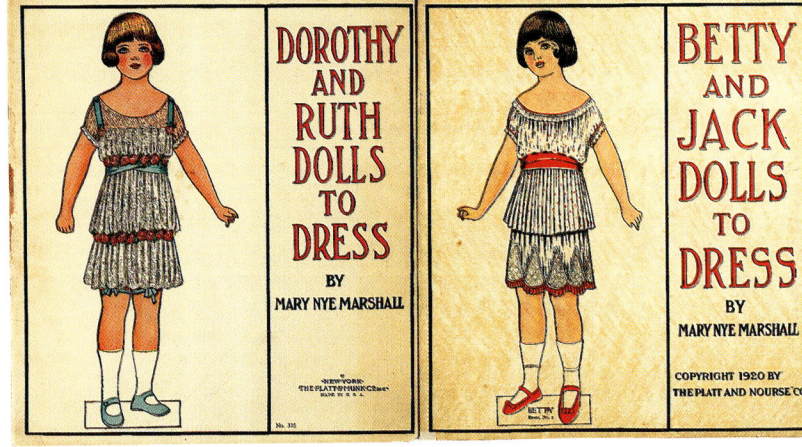

**263. Two American Paper Doll Books Designed by Mary Nye Marshall**
10" dolls. Two uncut books, 11" x 10", each feature a boy and girl paper doll on front and back covers, along with six uncut pages of costumes. Included are "Dorothy and Ruth" published by Platt and Munk, and "Betty and Jack" published by Platt and Nourse, dated 1920. Both designed by Mary Nye Marshall. Excellent condition. Circa 1920. $200/300

**265. Two American Paper Dolls by American Colortype with Slotted Hands** 12.5". Featuring Little Neddie Never-Still cut-out with easel-back, along with along sheet of uncut Little Neddie, 3 costumes including unusual swim suit with many plaything accessories such as sand pail, shovels, kite, fish net. And Little Willie Wide-Awake with two cut costumes, and one uncut sheet of Ski costume, along with many accessories and original colorful envelope noting that his hand is slotted so he can hold many playthings. Excellent condition. Circa 1910. $250/400

**266. Four Paper Dolls from American Colortype with Slotted Hands** each 12". Including uncut Little Polly Dress-up with three uncut sheets of costumes; Little Alice Busy Bee with 3 cut costumes and a wide variety of toys including sled and dog; uncut Little Betty Gad-About with one cut costume; and Miss Up-To-Date with 2 cut costumes and partial envelope. Each is designed with slotted hand to hold accessories. Excellent condition except typical envelope wear. Circa 1910. $250/400

Paper Dolls

**267. Large Group of Dennison Paper Dolls and Materials**
Including 8.5" "Nancy" with original envelope, instructions and pastel and patterned crepe paper, unplayed with; and another set with 12" "Eleanor" and 8.5" "Nancy" having instructions and a large number of printed double-sided uncut crepe paper costumes and materials. Also included is 7" boy. Each doll is fully-jointed at shoulders and hips. Dennison, circa 1920's. Excellent unplayed with condition throughout except wear to envelopes. $300/500

**268. Two Paper Doll Sheets "Lily" and "Bessie"**
3.5" x 6.5". Each is uncut punch-out style paper doll depicting a young child holding a doll or toy, marked Patent Pending and with name of child. Excellent condition, few tape marks at top edge. Circa 1920's. $100/150

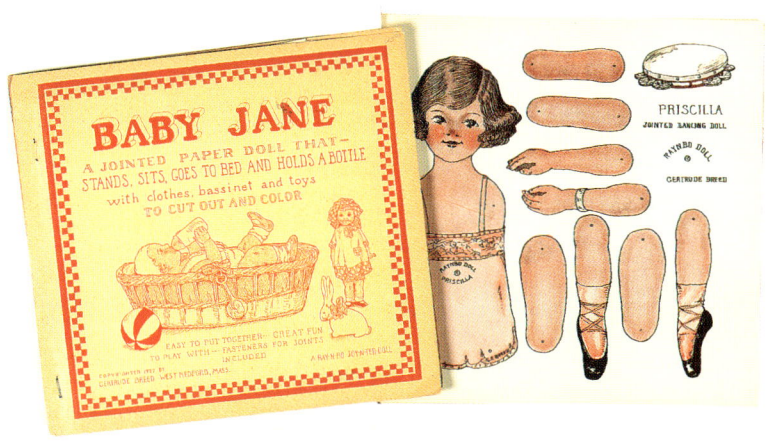

**269. Two American Paper Doll Books, "Baby Jane" and "Dancing Priscilla"**
Each 8" x 9" uncut sheets. "Baby Jane" includes uncut sheets of "a jointed paper doll that stands, sits, goes to bed and holds a bottle", and "Dancing Priscilla" includes uncut jointed doll along with pages to cut and color. Both have stapled covers, designed by Gertrude Breed, West Medford, Mass, "A Ray-N-Bo Joy-N-Ted Doll", copyright 1927. Excellent condition. $100/150

**270. American "Dolls To Cut Out" by American Colortype**
Includes four 12" cardboard cut-out dolls with easel back, and a large assortment of cut costumes and original packaging, along with uncut punch-out dolls "Georgie" and "Little Bob" with some cut costumes. Very good condition. Circa 1920's. $100/200

**271. American Paper Doll Book "Rag Doll Sue" by Harter**
13" x 9". With uncut profile paper doll on rear cover in stylized pose, and having eight pages of uncut costumes and accessories. Designed by Fern Bisel Peat, copyright 1931, The Harter Publishing Co, Cleveland. Excellent condition. $50/100

**272. American Paper Doll Book "Mother Goose" by Whitman**
13" x 9". Uncut book features five pages of punch-out dolls of nursery rhyme fame along with uncut costumes, in very stylized Art Moderne motif. Copyright 1937. Whitman Publishing. Excellent condition. $50/100

*Paper Dolls*

**273. American Paper Dolls Set "Olde Deerfield Dolls"**
Comprising two 22" x 10" panels of Old Deerfield Parsonage and Arosen's Wigwam to be used as scenery and six uncut sheets of paper dolls, each with three costumes depicting "Captives of 1704" rendered in delicate watercolors. Also included are six miniature books that match the persons shown in the paper dolls and telling their true historical tale. Drawings by Dorothy Epping Elliott. Copyright 1919. Excellent condition except wear to backgrounds. $400/500

***274. American Paper Doll Set by Margaret Price***
10" x 28" sheets. Two four-fold uncut sheets depict paper dolls "Davey", "Sue", "BabyCuddles" and "Priscilla" along with four costumes and accessories for each. Copyright 1920 by Margaret Evans Price. Excellent condition. 1920. $200/300

***275. German Paper Dolls by RAPL***
19" x 13". Four large uncut sheets on heavy pulp paper feature children in fashionable and traditional costumes. Drawn by Lungers Hausen. Published by Rapl in Germany. Sheets brittle at edges and upper right corner fading, overall good. Circa 1930's. $100/150

**276. American, Set of "Dollyland" Paper Dolls by Gabriel**
5.5". Six paper dolls including Pretty Pauline, Merry Marjorie, Sweet Sallie, Handsome Harold, Graceful Gertrude and Jolly Jack, each in its original envelope with variety of cut costumes and accessories. Also included is outer envelope "Dollyland, contains six different dolls", published and copyrighted by Gabriel. Excellent except worn outer envelope. Circa 1920. $150/200

### 278. American Uncut Paper Doll "Ruth" by Gabriel
10.5" x 8". An uncut light board sheet of young girl with four costumes and hats, labeled "Dolly Sheets, Ruth", copyright 1922 by Sam'l Gabriel. Excellent condition. Along with very brittle two pulp paper uncut sheets of Ruth (identical) and Nancy. Gabriel, 1922. $50/100

### 279. American Boxed Paper Doll "Wide Awake and Fast Asleep Doll Dorothy" by Gabriel
13" doll. Cardboard doll with jointing at shoulders and elbows, easel-back has mechanical sleeping eyes that operate to pushing and pulling hair bow. With four cut costumes and three hats, and original box with colorful lid. Sam'l Gabriel, patented USA, No. D 122. Excellent condition of costumes and doll, box lid vibrant albeit box sides flattened. Circa 1920. $100/200

### 277. American Paper Dolls "Brother Bob" and "Sister Nan" by Gabriel
each 9". Two cardboard cutout dolls with easel back depict young boy and girl, along with three costumes and three hats for girl, and four costumes and one hat for boy. With (flattened) original box for boy. Gabriel, circa 1920. Dolls and costumes excellent. $100/150

Paper Dolls

### 280. American Paper Doll Book "My Dollies" by Gabriel
11" x 16". Large stapled book has 2 uncut heavy sheets of paper dolls and costumes, comprising 9" Cousin Kate and Baby Betty, and 7.5" Alice and Dorothy, each doll with two costumes and two bonnets. Excellent condition. Copyright 1920 by Sam'l. Gabriel, New York. No. D-149. Excellent condition. $150/200

### 281. American Boxed "Happy Faces" Paper Dolls by Gabriel
10" doll. The box with colorful illustration on the lid, contains three interchangeable heads and one body, along with two cut costumes and two hats, and two sheets of uncut costumes. Gabriel, D-123, printed in Germany. Contents excellent, box spots and worn. Circa 1920. $100/150

**282. American Paper Doll Book "Fancy Dress Dolls" by Gabriel**
10.5" x 12.5". The staple bound uncut book features eight punch-out paper dolls with "novel costumes for all holidays and fancy dress parties". Designed by Betty Campbell. Gabride, No 896. Excellent condition. Circa 1930's. $100/150

**283. American Paper Doll Sheets from "Little Americans from Many Lands"**
10.5" x 8". Seven heavy paper sheets each feature one paper doll with four costumes (two of each costume are fashionable, two are traditional folklore type), along with flag from that country. Excellent condition. Circa 1920. $50/100

**284. Three Envelope Sets of "Twin Travelogues" by Abingdon Press**
9" x 7" books. Each set contains a book telling the story of the two paper dolls, and included are a wide selection of paper dolls and vignette scenes from each. Included is China, India and Japan. Designed by Welthy Honsinger, printed by Abingdon Press. Circa 1930's. Contents very good/excellent, envelopes ragged. $100/150

Paper Dolls 163

**285. American Paper Doll Book "Multi-Head Paper Dolls" by McLoughlin**
15" x 9.5" Staple-bound softbound book features two 15" paper dolls (boy and girl), each with six interchangeable heads, two interchangeable bodies, and two pages of uncut costumes and accessories. Copyright 1932 #542 McLoughlin Bros. Springfield. Excellent condition. $100/200

*286. American "Paper Playmates" by Volland*
6". Includes six cut paper dolls, 12 cut costumes, and 6 cut bonnets, all rendered in delicate pastel colors. With original glassene envelope labeled "Volland Paper Playmates and their Frocks". Published by P.F. Volland, Chicago, New York. Circa 1920. Dolls and costumes excellent, envelope has typical wear. $200/300

*287. American Paper Doll Book "Bettina and Her Playmate Rosalie" by Stecher*
18" x 10". A staple-bound softbound book with brilliantly colored cover features punch-out uncut paper dolls on front and back covers, along with two heavy cardboard punch-out uncut pages of costumes. Published by Stecher Lithograph of Rochester. Excellent condition. Circa 1920. $150/200

**288. American Paper Doll Book "Dollies to Dress Like Father and Mother"**
12" x 10". Staple bound, softbound book with stylized illustrations features 4 uncut paper dolls and uncut pages of costumes. Illustrated by Mary Nye Marshall, copyright 1917 by Platt and Nourse, with patent applied for concerning the "system for holding hats and hair pieces in place". Excellent condition. 1917. $150/200

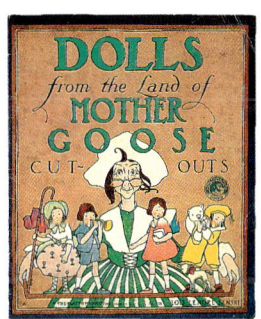

**289. Two American Paper Doll Books by Lois Lenski**
12" x 10". Each is staple-bound softbound book featuring fairy tale dolls in very stylized illustrations, including "Dolls from Fairyland" (copyright 1921 by Nourse Company, intact except one boy missing and a few costumes cut) and "Dolls from the Land of Mother Goose" (No221 by Platt & Munk. Complete and uncut). Both illustrated by Lois Lenore Lenski. Overall excellent, few bends on cover. 1921. $200/250

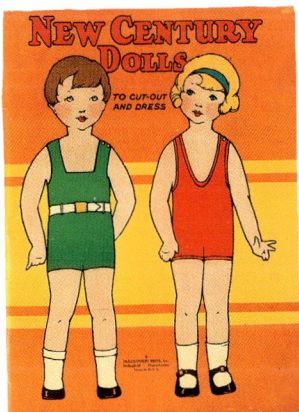

**290. American Paper Doll Book "New Century Dolls" by McLoughlin**
13" x 9". Staple-bound, softbound book features four double-sided 11" paper doll child along with 24 uncut pages of costumes. McLoughlin Bros, copyright 1929. Excellent condition. $100/200

*291. American Paper Doll Book "Adventures of Alice in Wonderland"*
12.5" x 10.5" Features punch-out stand-up figures of Alice and other characters in story settings, designed by Sidney Sage. The book is complete and intact. McLoughlin, No 964. Excellent condition. 1934. $100/200

*294. American Paper Doll Book "Dresses Worn by the First Ladies of the White House"*
11.5" x 13.5". The staple-bound, softbound book features four punch-out uncut slender ladies on the back cover, along with 11 pages of uncut costumes. Drawn by Maybelle Mercer, Saalfield, No 2164, 1937. Excellent condition. $100/200

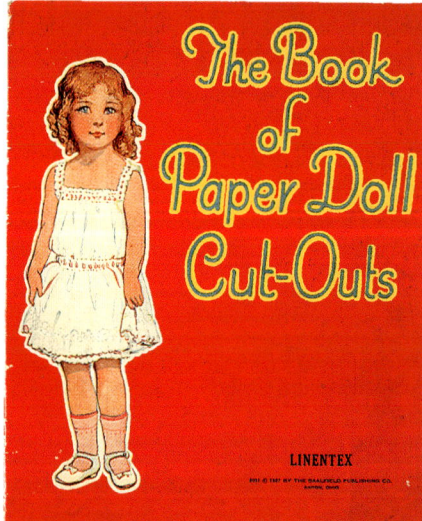

*295. American Paper Doll Book "Around the World"*
14" x 11". Featuring a variety of 9 cardbound punch-out uncut paper dolls and six pages of uncut costumes representing national costumes. Drawn by Dorothy Hoover Downs. No 2106, Saalfield, 1930's. Very good condition, some cover edge wear. $100/150

*292. American Paper Doll Book by Saalfield*
9" x 7.5". Of sturdy linen-like paper, trademarked "Linentex", the uncut book features four pages of paper dolls and costumes along with a storyline. Published by Saalfield. Very good/excellent condition. 1927. $50/100

**296. American Boxed Set of "Front and Back Paper Dolls" by Saalfield**
14" x 11" box. A cardboard box with colorful illustration of two paper dolls, contains both 13" double-sided paper dolls and 12 large uncut sheets of costumes. Saalfield, No. 233, copyright 1933. Contents excellent, some wear to box lid. $200/250

**297. Two American Paper Doll Books Drawn by Rachel Taft Dixon for Whitman**

Each 10" x 17". The flip-up books each contain 4 pages of uncut costumes, including "Historic Costumes", #906, with 8 paper dolls, and "Peasant Costumes of Europe", #900 (missing bottom costume decoration). Drawn by Rachel Taft Dixon. Whitman, 1934. $150/250

**299. American Paper Doll Book Designed Ruth E. Newton for Whitman**

10" x 17". Staple-bound softbound book features 12 cut-out pages of paper doll children and domestic animals, along with a cardboard page of toys and vignette settings such as bike ride, along with four further pages of uncut costumes. Drawn by Ruth E. Newton. Whitman, 1934. Excellent condition except fading strip at binding edge, and inscription on front cover dated 1939. $150/200

**298. American Paper Doll Book by Whitman**

12" x 7". Featuring two 11" punch-out uncut paper dolls on front and back covers and 4 uncut pages of costumes. Copyright 1932. Whitman. Excellent condition. $50/100

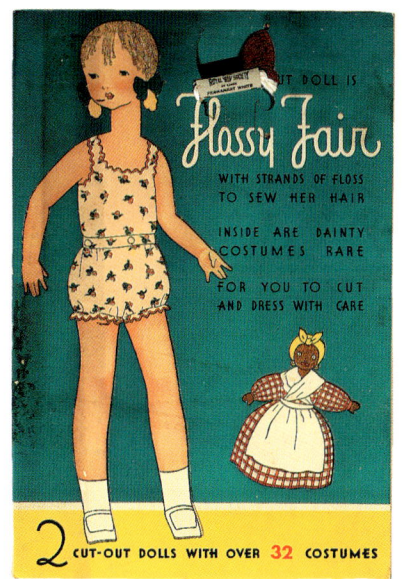

**300. American Paper Doll Book "Flossy Fair" by Whitman**
15.5" x 10.5". Staple-bound, softbound book features two double-sided 14" paper dolls of Flossy Fair and Peter Fair, along with punch-out doll or toy, and 5 pages of uncut costumes. The dolls were designed with floss thread to add to their heads in "wig" fashion, and the floss is still attached to the front cover. Whitman, 1933. Excellent condition. $100/150

**301. American Paper Doll Book "The Alden Family" Drawn by Frances Tipton Hunter**
13" x 10". The uncut book has beautifully illustrated cover depicting a child cutting paper dolls, and contains six child paper dolls with pages and punch-outs of numerous costumes and accessories. Complete and uncut. Whitman, 1943. $150/200

**302. American Paper Doll Book "Betty and Billy" by Whitman**
12" x 10" Featuring two punch-out paper dolls along with punch-out back cover of dog house, dog, dolls and toys, and six pages of costumes. Whitman, 1955, #2129. Excellent condition. $100/150

**303. American Paper Doll Book Design, Production Proof by Kathy Orr**
12" x 9". Production proof of "Bunny Paper Dolls" designed by Kathy Orr for Whitman, 1980, but never produced. Very good condition. $50/100

**304. American Paper Doll Book "Wedding of the Paper Dolls"**
17" x 10" Features 10 punch-out uncut paper dolls and six uncut pages of costumes, with vivid beautifully drawn cover design by Lucille Webster. Published by Merrill, M3487, circa 1939. Excellent condition except 1939 inscription on fron tcover. $100/150

Paper Dolls

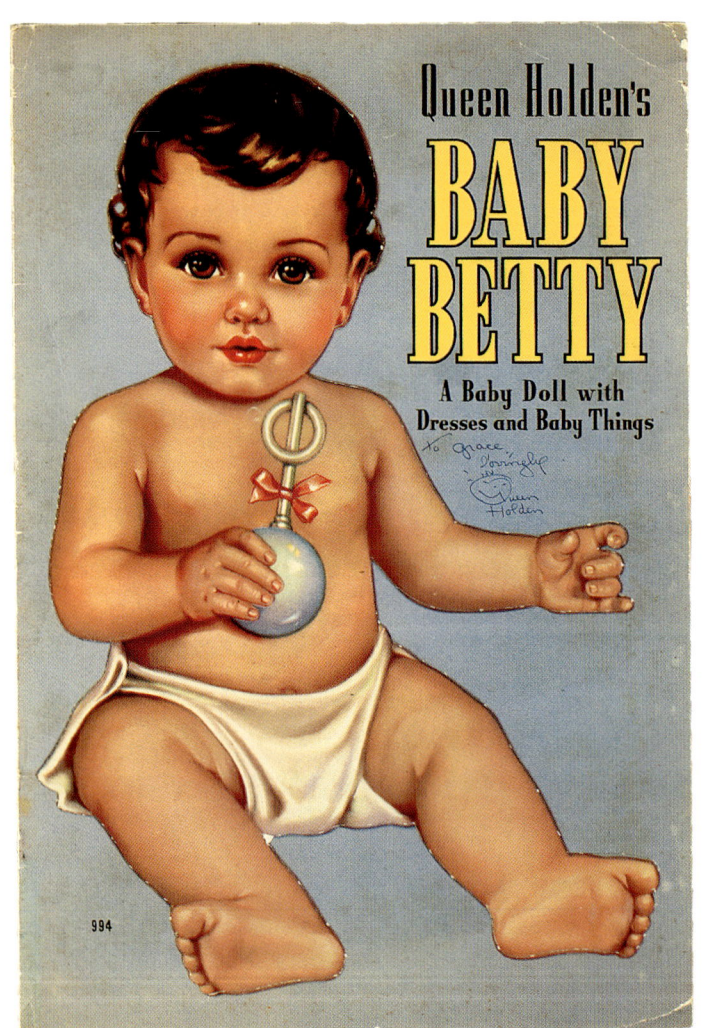

**306. American Paper Doll Book "Dress Me" by Queen Holden**
13" x 11". Cleverly designed front cover appears as though paper doll is peeking behind door. Featuring 14" punch-out paper doll with punch-out toys, 11" paper doll boy on back cover with more toys, and 4 pages of costumes. Whitman, 1943. Excellent condition. $200/300

**305. American Paper Doll Book "Baby Betty" with Queen Holden Autograph**
17" x 12". Featuring a large punch-out baby paper doll on front cover, and punch-out toys and accessories on back cover, along with five uncut pages of costumes and accessories. Designed by Queen Holden, published by Whitman, 1937, #994. The book is autographed on the front cover "Grace, Lovingly Queen Holden" with stylized Q. Excellent condition, upper right corner slightly bent. $200/300

**307. American Paper Doll Book "Baby Nancy" by Queen Holden**
12" x 12". Featuring front and back covers and four other pages of punch-out cardboard baby furniture, toys and accessories, along with 1 page of uncut paper costumes. Titled "Baby Nancy her Nursery and Clothes". Whitman, #W938, 1931. Excellent condition. $200/300

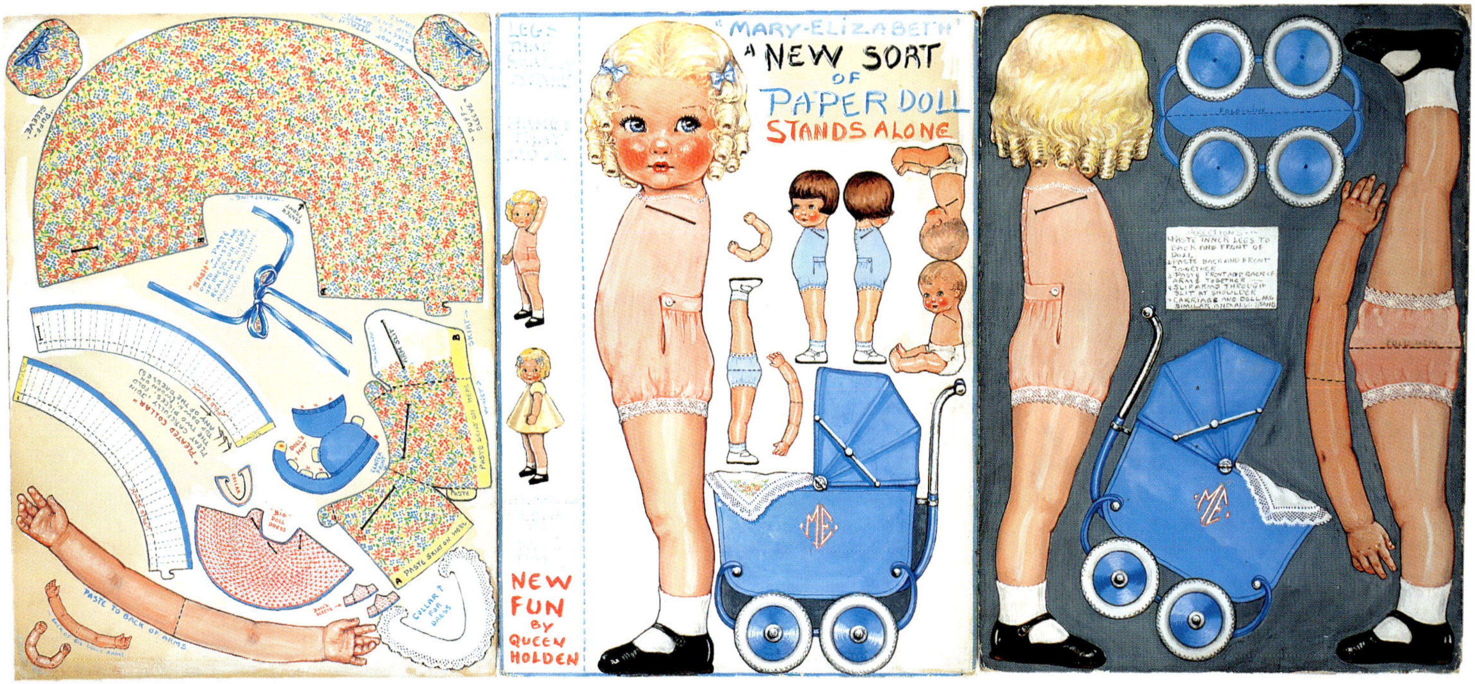

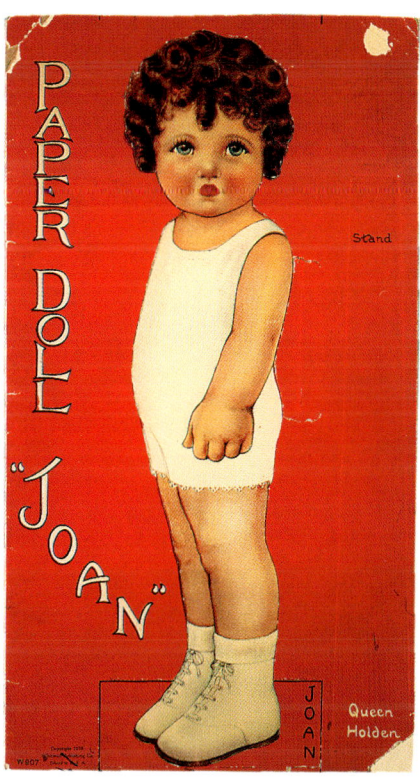

***308. Artist's Proof for "Mary-Elizabeth" Paper Doll by Queen Holden***
17.5" x 13". Featuring eight heavy art stock illustration boards with pastel illustrations of "A New Sort of Paper Doll" that stands alone, double-sided, with hands that move, all-around clothes, and many accessories. Includes directions for assembly of the clothes and the dolls. Designed by Queen Holden, a unique one-of-a-kind presentation of 8 boards. Circa 1940. Excellent condition. $400/600

***309. American Paper Doll Book "Glamour Girl" by Queen Holden***
15" x 10". Featuring profile paper doll that is partially shown on creatively designed front cover, along with punch-out accessories and dressing table on frontispiece and back cover and with six pages of uncut costumes and 20 different "hair-do's". Whitman, 1941. Excellent condition. $150/250

***310. American Paper Doll Book "Joan" by Queen Holden***
17" x 10". Featuring punch-out uncut paper dolls Joan and Bobby on front and back covers, along with six pages of uncut costumes and poems. Spine loose, dolls and costumes intact and fine. Whitman, 1928, W907. $100/150

Paper Dolls